Relentless

A Study for Those Called to Love

through Adoption & Foster Care

Relentless

A Study for Those Called to Love

through Adoption & Foster Care

Susan Killeen Jones, M.A., LPC, NCC

Roots & Wings Publishing

2018

First Printing: 2018

ISBN <Enter your ISBN> Roots & Wings Publishing

P.O. Box 761 Hillsboro, MO 63050

www.susankilleen.com Ordering Information:

Special discounts are available on quantity purchases by corporations, associations, educators, and others. For details, contact the publisher at the above listed address.

U.S. trade bookstores and wholesalers: Please contact Roots & Wings Publishing at 541-777-1543 or connect@susankilleen.com

Dedication

To my greatest teachers, my children.

I am forever changed, because you are mine.

Table of Contents

Preface

This book is written for those who have been called to be relentless in their pursuit to love a child beyond their own strength and ability. It is my hope that you will glean courage and joy from your own healing journey, so that you may parent from a wholehearted posture and truly be capable of changing the world for children.

"Indeed we call blessed those who showed endurance."
(James 5:11, NLT)

-Susan

Introduction

"It is impossible to win the race unless you venture to run, impossible to win the victory unless you dare to battle." - Richard M. DeVos

So often in life, our highest highs are quickly followed by our lowest lows. Dreams come true, but they don't always turn out to be quite what we'd hoped they might be. As an adoptive parent, you may have experienced this roller coaster. You may have enjoyed the climb toward your adoption goal. The journey may have even held several mountaintop experiences, but now you look around and find you're in a storm. You intended to make a difference in the world through parenting a child, but instead of feeling like you've reached your happy ending, you struggle to simply make it through the day.

Choosing to be an adoptive parent is like choosing to be a storm chaser, as you put yourself in a crazy position to experience unpredictable and sometimes powerful weather. We bravely, or naively, place ourselves in the chaos that has raged against children for generations: poverty, war, malnourishment, disease, abuse, and – worst of all – the apathy of adults around them. Parenting children with early life trauma and loss, can at times feel like experiencing a storm that never ends. It is a call to be relentless in loving children to healing, with unyielding courage and compassion.

This struggle is not only fought on an external level, focused on our children and their manifested set of issues. It is also an internal struggle we fight with ourselves, to choose to surrender our ways to something higher, committing to never give up the call on our lives. Relentlessly, we take a stand to love and serve a place of quiet strength that comes only from doing our own work first. This resolve requires us to acknowledge that we to, were once children, and our fight is similar to that of every child: to realize who we are and to Whom we belong. If we have any hope of helping our children navigate their journey, we must begin by healing the wounds of our own childhoods.

As an adoptive parent, you have many great resources already available to you, and I have no doubt you already have many of them in your hands. This book is not meant to replace those, but rather to compliment them by breaking down the barriers in ourselves that keep us from effectively implementing those tools. Many of us have experienced brokenness in our own past that has inflicted pain and wounds on our hearts, and influenced the shaping of our inner paradigms. When our pain collides with our children's pain, it's hard to love at all. It can feel like a continual battle. Like Paul, we find ourselves doing that which we don't want to do. As he writes, "I don't really understand myself, for I want to do what is right, but I don't do it. Instead, I do what I hate." (Romans 7:15, NLT) Even worse, we are unable to do what we know our kids need us to do. We have the tools to parent well, but are depleted of motivation or ability to use them.

Beyond practical insights and a new approach, my greatest desire is for this book to give you hope. You may be weary, but there is a way to refreshing and healing for your soul. I have written this book to remind you of your own needs and worth, as you consider the needs of your children. Let me be clear, I have walked where you are walking. It's not easy and I am the first to say that on my own, I've got nothin'. Yes, I have training, but mainly I'm just a mom that has been in the trenches for a while now. I've kept this book short and to-the-point (those of us who are using all we have just to make it to lunch, need it to be written that way.)

To facilitate the journey of inner healing this book is designed to take you on, there is a study guide at the end of each chapter to help you. The questions in this guide are best explored in the context of relationship and community. You may consider asking your own counselor, pastor, or support group to walk with you during this season.

Regardless of who you choose, it is vital you find someone who can relate to and respect your journey as an adoptive parent. As Dr. Dan Siegel states, "What is shareable, is bearable." Every adoptive parent has been relentless in their quest to save a child. What I'm asking of you now is to be equally relentless in the pursuit of yourself. God has a plan for you; seek it out with unyielding fervor.

-Susan

Chapter 1

Great Expectations

"The first time I saw a picture of my daughter she was wearing soiled pants. Her expression reflected fear, but also fierce determination. I was reminded of that image months later when during her tantrums she would threaten, 'I'm gonna pee!' It had been her best defense and method of control so far in her young life, and it was not a tool she was willing to give up easily."

-Sarah, P.

"Aint no Mountain High Enough"

Few of us plan to struggle. That would be lunacy. No, we start out with great intentions of doing well and living well. Every parent I've met wants to succeed in having a happy family and helping their children thrive. Yet, for those of us raising children with developmental trauma, the goal of living well can seem impossibly out of reach. I've heard of this type of parenting in a complex family, compared to taking an AP course in school. While chemistry is difficult in and of itself, AP chemistry is much tougher and should only be attempted by those who are willing to work!

Adoptive families must face added complexities, and are assigned a course they may not be equipped to pass. There is no shame in not being properly equipped to flawlessly navigate being an adoptive parent. Maybe you were never told how difficult it might be. Maybe you were warned, but your rose colored glasses dismissed the warning that might have caused you to prepare better. Or maybe you prepared the best you could, but brought home a child with bigger than ordinary challenges. Regardless of the reason, you're here. You have chosen to love your child, a child who will require much from you.

Children who have endured early life trauma or loss, need parenting founded in relentless love that goes beyond what is common in traditional parenting. Early life circumstances have placed these kids at risk for wounded hearts and minds; developmental processes have often been interrupted, leaving them ill equipped to cope with the magnified issues that are facing them. In order to give children the intensive care they require, parents must first examine the condition of their own hearts and minds. Effective healing in our children, begins and flows from healing in our own lives. You may not realize some of the areas of brokenness that need to be addressed. Ask yourself these questions with an open mind, noting the ones you identify with:

- Is there any part of me that is angry and disappointed?

- Am I weary from exhaustion?

- Has my heart become unfaithful due to constant exposure to conflict and chaos?

- Have I become stuck in unforgiveness, which steals my attention and energy?

- Is my heart fearful or bitter?

- Do I think of the future with worry and doubt things could ever change?

Asking yourself these questions (and others like them) will help you determine where your heart may be wounded, so you can pursue healing in that place. To make peace with where we are, we may need to rewind and examine what we thought life would look like as an adoptive parent. Expectations are only natural, but as we've all experienced, they can rob us of so much joy. It's time to get honest and peel back the layers of our unmet expectations, and acknowledge the circumstances that may have caused us to have those expectations in the first place. Let's examine some of the most common reasons I've encountered of why parents choose to adopt.

Reason #1: Infertility, Miscarriage, and Loss

For many, experiencing the loss of a child provides a situation that prompts them to adopt. Parents often choose to grow their family through adoption after a season of infertility and loss through miscarriage. I have even seen the loss of a sibling in childhood become the precursor for adoption. The longing to replace tragedy with joy can be fierce . . . and desperate. There is a very real potential for unresolved grief to give way to unhealthy motives and unrealistic expectations. I once counseled a woman who turned down several referrals from her agency, saying each child didn't fit the vision she had for the child she wanted to adopt. The agency asked me to intervene as something felt "off" in the situation. Upon further inquiry, I learned she had suffered multiple miscarriages, and envisioned adopting a blonde-haired, blue- eyed child. Strangely though, she was on the wait list to adopt from Guatemala. Clearly, she had expectations based more on her personal loss than the reality of her program of choice.

It is tempting to ignore the effort required to work through grief, and focus on replacing the pain with a different outcome. Let me be clear though: adoption is no substitute for working through your grief. That said, there is nothing inherently wrong with adopting after a loss. My own miscarriage gave way to starting conversations of adopting. I am simply saying that grief can be a monster, and unless it is dealt with, the consequences can wreak havoc in a family. Your job is to honestly evaluate the thoughts and feelings concerning your loss, and determine if your expectations have been wrongly influenced by unresolved grief. If it was, take time to work through the pain now, as you gently untangle it from your present circumstances.

Reason #2: To Evangelize a Child

In working with adoptive parents, one motivation for adoption I've heard is evangelism. These parents' main reason for wanting to adopt was to see that child convert to Christianity, with the hope they will eventually return to their birth country as a Missionary. Adopting with this intent is, in my opinion, not exactly what Jesus meant when He told us to go share the good news. I believe it is unfair to place that kind of expectation on any child, and doing so will ultimately do more damage than good. While it may be a beautiful thing for adopted children to return to their country of birth and share the love of Christ, it is certainly no reason to adopt.

This vision of evangelism should be something that happens naturally, through the overflow of a lifetime of being well-loved by a family motivated by a desire to parent and love unconditionally. A child's future belongs to them. Placing expectations on a child to become an evangelist may set a family on a direct path to a lot of pressure, stress, and potential rebellion.

Sadly, this performance-based parenting can lead to an attitude of conditional love and acceptance. If you pursued adoption from this desire, take a step back and reevaluate this motivation. Remind yourself your child needs to know you love them for who they are, not for what they can do. No child – adopted or biological – should be pressured by their parent, to become that parent's idea of who they should be. Children should be loved and freed to be the amazing people God has designed them to be, and encouraged to pursue the future He has for them. Love them, dream with them, and then watch their lives unfold from your nurture and support.

Reason #3: To Provide a Sibling

A common reason well-meaning parents choose to adopt is for the sole purpose of providing a sibling for their existing child or children. Often, these parents approach the adoption agency with a wish list that sounds like they are ordering from a menu: "We have children of these ages, so we would like a boy of such-and-such age and a girl between the ages of such-and-such to play with our kids." There have been moments I have wanted to respond, "Would you like fries with that?" I feel so convinced that we should be finding families for children and not children for families.

While often siblings (by birth or adoption) do become close friends, this isn't always the case. The risk for families adopting with this motivation is that the sibling relationship turns out less than ideal. A family can quickly discover that to their existing child, an adopted sibling can become like the friend you wish would leave already. An adopted child should not come home to expectations that he or she will be a swell brother/sister/friend/plaything. On the other side of the coin, your existing children should not be forced to carry the weight of such huge, life-changing decisions such as adoption. Relationships are challenging, siblings need to be prepared for the many changes and sacrifices coming their way. Release your expectations of both children, and focus instead on creating a strong, healthy, and safe family environment, where relationships can naturally build. Be ready to offer customized parenting as children often require different parenting skills.

Reason #4: Dream to Parent through Adoption and Foster Care

Occasionally, I have come across a person who says they have always known being an adoptive parent was their destiny, since the time they were a young child. The risk for this person is an over-romanticized childhood dream that doesn't match the sometimes difficult reality of their experience. If adoption was chosen out of an idealistic desire to rescue a child, versus providing years of restorative parenting, the family has potentially set themselves and their child on a path headed for heartache. There is nothing wrong with having a dream to adopt, but it's very important for you to purposefully seek out the truth of adoption, realizing you won't have a perfect "happily ever after" story without some bumps and challenges along the way. Again, the culprit here is having unrealistic expectations.

The second risk is a spouse who may or may not have shared the same level of commitment to the dream of adoption. If they had this childhood desire forced upon them by their spouse, resentment may not be far behind. Parenting a child through adoption requires an unbelievable amount of commitment and engagement from both parents.

If one spouse wasn't completely on board with the idea in the first place, they are likely to experience strong negative emotions when the going gets tough. This, in turn, can put the unity of your marriage in jeopardy. If you are a couple in this situation it may prove beneficial to seek outside counsel. It is important that you have an honest discussion and move toward forgiveness and support of one another.

It is vital that every child have parents that are committed to their care and progress. Couples may need a seasoned marriage therapist to help them heal their relationship, while building strong communication skills and parenting strategies.

Reason #5: Obedience Equals Reward

Some of us think if we do the "right thing" in this world, we will be rewarded. We have been trained that in life, obedience equals reward or "do good; get good." We are the achievers: the ones who sit near the front of the class and always try to be on time.

We have bought in to the theory, if you obey the rules and sacrifice for others, a personal happy ending is in store. We don't necessarily think of ourselves as performers, but rather have a sincere desire to please the Lord and do what He says. While not necessarily "doing good" purely for the sake of the reward, at some level we do expect things to go well for us. Secretly, we like it when others applaud our efforts and find it crushing when we find ourselves standing alone with few who understand our struggles. If we are honest, we also find ourselves struggling to understand God and His ways over our own.

The key to enduring this is reframing our idea of suffering, and making peace with the truth. Of course, as we know all too well, what goes around doesn't always come around. Bad things happen to good people, and seemingly undeserving people get off the hook. We may not have a "happily ever after" ending the way we expect it, but there is happiness, joy, peace, and contentment to be found, as we identify with Christ and shift focus to gratitude. If this is you, take time to talk to God and share your frustrations and disappointment. Get honest. Do you feel tricked by God? Do you feel somehow cheated or mislead by years of instruction that gave you this mindset?

Expectations Meet Reality

Regardless of the motivations that led you to adopt, at some point your expectations will collide with reality. The good news is, some aspects of adoption may exceed your expectations, and there will be many happy moments and memories. However, if you are reading this book, it's likely because you have discovered there are also unexpected challenges. I commonly interact with parents who have spent hours poring over photos and blogs on the Internet that only portray the smiling, happy side of being an adoptive family. Seeing this seemingly perfect "reality," parents start to wonder, "Why is our family different?" and ask, "Are we the only ones who are struggling?"

It reminds me of our recent family move to the Northwest. When sharing with a family member how tough the transition had been and how homesick I felt, she replied, "Well, your sister showed me your photos on Facebook and you all sure seem happy." I wanted to reply,

"Well, I guess we're just not posting many shots of us crying or fighting these days." Social media is great at helping us put on a happy face for the world. The trouble is how quickly it turns into a dangerous land mine for comparison. We all tend to put our best foot forward in front of other people, and online it's especially easy to hide the "ugly" parts of life. Even if an adoption blog shares the hard parts of the journey, it's still too easy for the author to gloss over it and lessen the harshness of the reality. These fairy-tale versions of adoption can give pre-adoptive parents expectations of complete happiness, and seamless transitions post-adoptions, just like what they've read online or seen at the airport. They think, "We will be happy; our child will be happy!" They may even go so far as to think, "Our child will be grateful. Yes; we will have a happy, grateful child!" Then, when the tough times come, these parents are sideswiped and flabbergasted their reality doesn't live up to their expectation.

Parents need to know that some, if not all of our expectations about parenting will be challenged at one point or another. The expectations of our outcome, expectations of our responses, and even our expectations of God will all come under fire. In fact, it's highly likely at some point you or your spouse will say things like, "What have we done? I didn't sign up for this! Where is God? How will we survive this? Did we misunderstand the call? This feels impossible!" In the midst of asking questions like these, adoptive families desperately need the support of their Christian communities, and yet, too many of us hang back hiding out of a sense of false shame. Though often the children in their care come home with wounded hearts and minds, others have looked at them as if they are the problem. As parents, we frequently hold our children out as mirrors to our worth, competency, and value. When our kids look and act a mess, it leaves us feeling like at some level we are failures. We are sensitive to comments, looks, and judgements of others. At times we want to carry around a disclaimer, "She came to us this way!" Though we long for connection, we are fearful of our vulnerable status. We carry the burdens of every orphan child, and somehow believe that if the rest of the world knew just how hard this was, they would never adopt. Children would be left abandoned and parentless . . . it would be on us.

Sometimes parents find the courage to share and be open about their struggles, only to be met with criticism and confusion, even from their own extended families. These well-meaning friends and family members think, "After all, they chose this for themselves, right?" That attitude causes adoptive parents to isolate themselves even more from others, leaving them left to question their sanity alone. Feeling like no one is there to understand, can at times even begin to cause people to distance themselves from God. Slowly, like a wall going up brick by brick, a depressed and frustrated attitude builds total self-reliance and an angry heart.

The stress and the pain of it all can tear at the fragility of a couple's marriage. Where there is weakness, there will be testing. Not all adoptive parents will make it. Some will quit. It will be too much for them. Their mental and emotional frameworks will come under attack, and sadly they will break. They will leave their families and abandon their role as a parent. It will be up to the rest of us to relentlessly stand for the children left behind.

For this and other reasons, the sense of overwhelm will be fierce. You may feel alone, crazy, and beyond stressed. However, to any parent who is experiencing this, I say this: You are normal. Everything is alright. God is big enough to handle your questions, and welcomes the conversation. Don't stop going to Him. Listen to hear Him saying, "Bring it all to Me . . . your fears, anger, frustration, and exhaustion. My mercies are new every day, My grace is sufficient for you. I will accomplish My purposes through you, mighty warrior; fight from My strength and not your own."

Our God is an intimate Father who wants us to hold nothing back. He is ready, willing, and able to meet you where you are, or wherever you may find yourself in the future. He is there to reveal more of Himself to you in every situation you encounter. In His amazing grace, He can use your frustrations to heal the brokenness and false beliefs of your own life experience. He is here, and He sees you. Keep trying. Be honest with yourself, and keep trying to find at least one other person you can be honest with.

I am confident the best method to begin healing pain is by bringing it into the light of God's love. "Such love has no fear, because perfect love expels all fear. If we are afraid, it is for fear of punishment, and this shows that we have not fully experienced his perfect love." (1 John 4:18, NLT) What good news this is to us as believers! When our hearts are failing us, we can look to the One whose love is perfect. We allow Him to heal our hearts first, so we can become more like Him to our children. The best parents are not perfect, but instead draw strength and virtue from their perfect Father. God can restore our hearts, allowing us to be parents who are positioned to give love freely, having placed our own disappointments and pain in His   hands

Chapter 1 Study
Great Expectations

1. Discuss your adoption story. What prompted you to consider adoption?

2. Do you remember being excited? What were your expectations?

3. What role did God play in your decision to adopt?

4. Were there times of fear and challenge along the way? Discuss.

5. In what ways did God show His faithfulness?

6. How has your faith been challenged since you came home?

7. In an attempt to manage our pain, we often use coping mechanisms in some way. Consider the following and write about how you have experienced each in your situation.

Denial/Masking (pretending everything is okay)

Rationalization (minimizing your experience/feelings)

Suppression (conscious attempt to avoid your thoughts and feelings)

Isolation (withdrawal from people and activities)

Bargaining (if . . . then . . . thinking)

Imploding (physical symptoms such as headaches, sleeplessness, muscle tension, jaw clenching etc.)

Exploding (outbursts of anger, tears, overall irritability) - What would your family say of these?

Outward Coping Behaviors (smoking, drinking, over-spending, over-eating, over-sleeping)

8. If you have tried to reach out to others, what has been their reaction? Where have you found support?

9. You may have uncovered many new insights about yourself and your strategies of surviving in the valley. What was the most profound insight you had? If you could ask God one question about your situation, what would it be?

Chapter 2

The Hole

"My child cries . . . no, my child wails. She is heartbroken and I can do nothing. I am helpless. Frustrated. Exhausted."

-Julie, R.

"There's a Hole in my Bucket Dear Liza"

Do you remember the little song about Liza, Henry, and the hole in the bucket? Liza tells Henry to "mend it," as if the situation were a no-brainer. He uses straw, but it is too long. She tells him to cut it with a knife, but the knife is dull. Liza continues by telling Henry to sharpen the knife. He needs a stone to sharpen the knife, but the stone must be wet first; to fetch the water, Henry needs the bucket but, alas, there's a hole in the bucket! In the words of my Jewish Grandmother, "Oy vey!" What a nauseating, frustrating little song. But it paints a vivid picture of the frustrating cycle many of us find ourselves stuck in. Have you ever felt this way? It seems like the situation should be easy to repair, but nothing seems to go right. All your efforts fall flat, you can't catch a break, and exchanges that should be simple are excruciatingly difficult. This vicious cycle quickly becomes a common theme.

I remember my friend and former boss, Frank Block, once telling me that most people who are drawn into the world of orphan care very often have childhood issues of their own to explore. He shared it with me as if giving me a friendly warning. In retrospect of my personal story, I have to agree. On some level, identifying with hurt and vulnerable children has been an attempt at healing my own childhood pain. There is a deep place in me driving this passion. I want to mend the hole of injustice, loss, and pain because I understand it from a place of experience. I can relate. I am passionate about helping others notice the hole, and moving them to do something about it. However, I have learned – the hard way, I might add – that the best way I can help my children, is to pursue healing in myself first.

The problem with this scenario is many of us are trying to give our children traits that we ourselves lack. We want them to be content, joyful, loving and kind. Yet, we worry, stress, and find ourselves lacking in so many areas. Like the airline message goes, we need to secure our own oxygen mask before helping our children. Did you ever stop to think about why they say this? In an airline emergency, without securing their own oxygen mask first, a parent would quickly be rendered useless. They would most likely pass out before helping their children get their mask on, leaving the kids helpless, at risk, and with little hope of survival. What an appropriate picture of how we parent when we don't choose to address our own brokenness first! It's exactly what we do when we struggle to be so child-focused, we are useless in any real sense because we simply cannot do it on our own. We are left passed out in the aisle as our children gasp for air.

Many of us could give workshops on the effects of malnutrition, sensory integration, and causes of attachment disorder, yet find ourselves failing at home with our children. We do everything we can to figure out how to patch the hole in our children by reading an abundance of books, attend seminar after seminar, and track down every last online chat group, website, or blog that might offer insight. But in the midst of this laser-focused pursuit of healing for our children, what are we doing to strengthen ourselves? Does knowledge and theory make a difference if our own brokenness keeps us from applying that knowledge? If we are only working from an external perspective rather than an internal conviction, how can we expect to be truly impactful? When our children's behavior triggers our own ingrained negative reactions, we can't truly be the parents they require. It is up to us to honestly explore our own deep places so that we can do better for our children . . . and ourselves.

A lot of parents, especially moms, will share many excuses why they do not engage in self-exploration and care. I often hear one or more of the following:

- There's not enough time.

- It's too expensive.

- The whole idea is scary.

- Been there; done that.

- What's the point?

- I can press through; I'll be fine.

- I need to focus on my kids.

I want to support you, and gently admonish you to do it anyway. Your emotional health and self-awareness is vital to living well, and providing the tools your children need to thrive. I welcome and encourage you to engage in the journey of self-exploration and spiritual revelation. Perhaps your struggles will give you reason to overcome your barriers for such a time as this. Parenting through challenging situations can often be an avenue that God uses to reflect the character of Christ. It's a hidden gift few of us would enlist to pursue, if we were given full disclosure up front of what it would take to receive it. Nevertheless, it is a gift of the journey. I have often said that parenting through adoption feels as if it is more about the sanctification of parents, than it is the journey of a child into a family. Of course, it is both, but many fail to realize parenting holds many life lessons for the parents. It isn't just about the children. It's a humbling journey that can lead parents to an intimate knowledge of Christ like no other.

I firmly believe parenting that heals, begins with healed parents. Children are most impacted by parents who are experienced in the healing process because of their own journey through it; those who parent from the inside out, with oxygen masks fully secured and seat belts on. It is completely possible to make sincere internal changes in order to parent more effectively from a place of wholeness that benefits not only our children, but also richly blesses our own lives.

A Word about Being a Warrior

My friend, Sharon, once told me she had so many groundhogs on her family's property they were actually destroying her family's large barn. If you are unfamiliar with these little guys, let me introduce you. They are giant rodents that appear to be the cousin of the beaver, minus the tail. In the words of Wikipedia, "Groundhogs are excellent burrowers, using burrows for sleeping, rearing young, and hibernating. The average groundhog has been estimated to move approximately 35 cubic feet (710 pounds) of soil when digging a burrow. Groundhog burrows usually have two to five entrances, providing groundhogs their primary means of escape from predators. Burrows are particularly large, with up to 46 feet of tunnels buried up to five feet underground." Essentially, they are moles on steroids. Sharon can tell you stories of horses, kittens, and people who have been injured on her family farm after falling into one of these burrows. While accidents like this were common, a collapsing structure was another story.

To the untrained eye, Sharon's barn looked fine. A traditional Kentucky barn, it seemed to showcase strong rafters and solid walls that had hosted season after season of tobacco farming. Yet underneath the surface, groundhogs were tunneling to such a great extent that the barn was losing all stability. It was going to collapse without intervention. Having grown up on a farm, Sharon had been trained and knew just what to do: She grabbed her gun and went out Annie Oakley-style. My friend was on a mission to reclaim what had been in her family for generations, and was now being stolen. An excellent shot, we came to call her "the Groundhog Slayer."

Many of us know that feeling of suiting up for battle. Yet the long-term work of healing the broken places in children, and in ourselves, is a different issue involving solutions more complex than a shotgun. You are not a Christian Super Hero who has come to save the day – Jesus already has that role in the story. Your role is to participate with Him in the process. The enemy is absolutely out to take that which is most precious to God. Satan has plans; he moves his arm of rodent-like soldiers with the focused intent of tearing down children and families. He means to crumble the foundation of society, bringing communities and nations down with them. And he is not likely to surrender his plans easily.

The truth is, we begin our role with these children with great passion. They are the dreams in our hearts, the physical representation of love that impassions us to cross mountains of paperwork, overcome financial barriers, and bridge cultural divides. Through the eyes of our hearts we see our children's futures: they are days filled with health, joy, and goodness. We firmly believe this passionate love we hold is God-given, and has the supernatural ability to override anything our children, or the generations before them have had to endure. How can we be so right and so wrong at the same time? Yes, this incredible love driving us to adoption is God-given, because God Himself is love. We read, "Anyone who does not love does not know God, for God is love." (1 John 4:8, NLT) We are arrogant and wrong to think this love originates in us, or that we can sustain it on our own. How can we think once we fall in love with a child that love will remain without a fight? Our minds and hearts come to this conclusion when loving is easy. Falling in love with a newborn, for example, feels natural and effortless. I have to smile when a baby first comes home too tired to even cry, and the new parent proudly boasts, "She's a really good baby!" That tune is quickly changed when the crying and four a.m. feeding become commonplace. However, when this shift occurs, something powerful happens: sacrificial love begins to kick in. This is the love we give when it hurts. Love that is patient and kind to a little needy baby who can give nothing in return.

For most adoptive parents, falling in love with the idea of parenting a child who needs them is easy. Our hearts are full of compassion and love even before we meet our child. It's similar to what God does through the process of pregnancy, preparing the heart to love deeply and sacrificially. This "infatuation" love fuels our journey of pursuing and finding our child, but it isn't enough to carry you through the next phase of the journey.

Loving children who not only do not return our affection, but also reject or hurt us repeatedly and even intentionally requires much more. This enduring love goes beyond common experience, and is built on sacrifice and service going above and beyond. It is harder for our brains to comprehend this love, and what it will require of us.

The best way I know how to describe the love it takes to parent children who can be difficult, is like placing your hand over a burner on the stove with the instructions, "When you feel the heat, press down." Our logical brains can't compute this directive; it wants to override the command, withdrawing to protect. This isn't bad – it's how God designed our brains. Yet, it is all too easy to let this natural self-preservation mode become our common pattern. If we aren't mindful of allowing God to soften our hearts and teach us to love with His love, we will get stuck operating from this pattern by default.

It is the same when we consider healing our own pain and histories of trauma. Healing requires that we press into the pain, over-riding the logical brain at times, and relentlessly and mindfully going deeper into the truth of our stories. If we can do that, we can help our children do the same.

Breathe

You must learn to breathe, for it is your birthright and a great tool for conquering fear and stress. Breath is our teacher as well. It can tell us when we are being triggered and in fear, before we may even know why. Pay attention to it. Learn to use it to calm your nervous system, and find the ground beneath you. Too many of us are satisfied with catching short breaths as we strive to go faster and faster. Imitating swimmers we gasp for air and then quickly return our focus to the race before us. We push ourselves harder and harder, and isolate ourselves to our own lane. We don't want to appear weak, but in the process lose our opportunity to pace ourselves and find balance.

Returning to our illustration of the airline breathing masks, I have to admit I've always thought those oxygen masks were so ugly. I don't mean "ugly" as a fashion statement, I mean "ugly" in scary, end-of-the-world, creepy sense. They appear confining and leave me feeling like I can't breathe just looking at them. It's hard to believe they could be helpful, let alone lifesaving. Personal healing of the heart can be like that too. It requires actions that are unfamiliar and scary. Trust and vulnerability are vital. Like oxygen masks, you have to put them on and leave them on, no matter how foreign and awkward you may feel. Disengaging early means devastation to you and those depending on you.

Imagine you're in an aircraft and the cabin pressure suddenly changes, causing those awful oxygen masks to fall from their compartments overhead. Could you see yourself remaining in complete denial in that situation, pretending like nothing was wrong in an effort to maintain self-sufficiency? Probably not! Then why do we remain so stubborn about the challenges in front of us as parents? If parenting is hard, and adoption is hard, why would we think parenting adopted children would be easy? It only stands to reason it would be difficult.

As I mentioned before, I greatly underestimated the challenge in front of me when I adopted. My two biological kids were pretty easy and very enjoyable to parent, and arrogantly I thought it had everything to do with me. I believed I was a great mom who could handle any kid from any circumstances. With a little preparation, what could be so hard about adoption? After all, I was a counselor and educator – for adoptive families, no less! I thought I had this thing down. I couldn't have been more wrong. Initially, it was incredibly tough to admit we were struggling. I know what it feels like, not being able to breathe, feeling out of control and afraid of crashing. I have felt that "cabin pressure failure" feeling in our home too many times to count. I know why my kids hoard food, rage for hours, run away, steal, and lie to my face. I could give, and have given seminars on the reasons and theories, but none of that has meant much to me when I've been buried in the midst of a storm. During those times it was difficult to breathe and easy to panic.

After enduring so many downpours, anxiety began to feel normal, giving way to exhaustion, apathy, and defeat. The time came that I recognized many of my struggles were pointing to my own childhood "hole." Somehow, all of this was related. I had to get honest, with myself and with God. I had many ugly cries and conversations with Him, as I learned to trust Him more with my brokenness and feelings of being out of control. I pressed in to His promises, met with a trusted counselor, and had a dear friend go to war with me through prayer, again and again. I learned to fast and pray, and battle the tapes in my head victoriously. I studied everything I could get my hands on to help heal my kids, and internalized the lessons for myself. It took a long time of persistence to get even the smallest movement, yet my family situation gave me little choice but to continue falling on my face in need of God and a better way to live.

If you are suffering in your situation, I can imagine the many questions playing in your head: "Why me? How could this happen? Who am I now? When will it get better?" I find a story from the 31st chapter of Deuteronomy greatly encouraging. In this story, you will find Moses speaking to the Hebrew people. The people were nervous and afraid as they stood on the brink of stepping into a new land, a Promised Land. In that new land, there were many enemies to be defeated (as you know, even good change can be stressful!) There was also something else though. Moses, who was now 120 years old and had been the people's leader for 40 years, was passing on leadership to his successor, Joshua. The theme of Moses' command is very clear in this chapter, and in the following pages at the beginning of the book of Joshua. We read, "So be strong and courageous! Do not be afraid and do not panic before them. For the Lord your God will personally go ahead of you. He will neither fail you nor abandon you." (Deuteronomy 31:6, NLT)

John tells a similar story. Jesus is preparing His beloved disciples for His departure. He promises them He is going ahead to prepare a place for them, and then speaks words consistent with the command of Deuteronomy: "Don't let your hearts be troubled. Trust in God, and trust also in me." (John 14:1, NLT) In other words, "Be strong and courageous." This time though, there is an added promise to the command: "No, I will not abandon you as orphans—I will come to you. Soon the world will no longer see me, but you will see me. Since I live, you also will live." (John 14:18, NLT) Jesus promises that He will not forsake us, but that He will live in us and enable us to be strong and courageous.

While I believe these passages motivate us toward faith, I also believe our faith and decision for courage starts with breath. God designed our bodies to fight stress through breath. The very word 'breath' in the Hebrew is the same word for "life' and name of the Holy Spirit. "Ruach" meaning 'air in motion' is worth noting. Our best weapon against panic is to breathe with intention and focus on God.

What are the messages you listen to? During the tough times of suffering, grief, and disappointment, it's tempting to lose sight of God's promises, and hard to find breath. When you feel beaten like the Scarecrow in *The Wizard of Oz* after a battle with winged monkeys, the lies of the enemy seem reasonable and real. You can feel like he did, "There's a piece of me over there, and some of me over here!" It is unsettling at best, and the world is quick to insert its own wisdom into our situation: "Fake it 'til you make it." some say, "Others have it much worse." Others say such things as, "Grin and bear it." or, my personal favorite, "Suck it up buttercup." You might even be told to "Make the best of it." and "Pull yourself up by your bootstraps." I'm here to tell you these maxims are not only harmful, but a dangerous way to live.

It's tempting to resort to defense mechanisms to survive the storm, to escape the situation by trying to rely on your own strength to make it through. The truth is though, God doesn't want us to merely survive our storm; He wants to give us victory in that place. He goes before us, He is with us, and nothing can separate us from His love. As Paul promises, "I am convinced that nothing can ever separate us from God's love. Neither death nor life, neither angels nor demons, neither our fears for today nor our worries about tomorrow— not even the powers of hell can separate us from God's love." (Romans 8:38, NLT)

If you're feeling stuck without the ability to breathe, let me encourage you and remind you that you have been placed in this role for such a time as this. It is no accident you find yourself where you are today. No matter how you received this assignment of loving your child with extraordinary love, it is your task to complete this journey well. Will you take the necessary steps to care for yourself first, so you can better care for your children? This is your time to engage in the unknown, place yourself in a process of vulnerability that may seem scary, and face the rain.

Chapter 2 Study
The Hole

Freely and honestly finish the following sentences:

I am afraid that_____

_____

I wish that_____

_____

I don't understand_____

_____

I want_____

_____

I am angry that_____

_____

If only_____

_____

Why can't I_____

_____

How long must I_____

_____

When will_____

_____

I need_____

_____

I dislike_____

_____

I am confused by_____

_____

I am concerned that_____

_____

Where_____

_____

I long for_____

_____

I am ashamed_____

_____

I feel guilty that_____

_____

I desire_____

_____

I should_____

_____

If only I could_____

_____

I have to_____

_____

      What feelings come up for you in this exercise? Take a moment to breath (In for 7 and out for 11) Cry if you need to, and sit still for 5 minutes focusing on nothing but your breath . . . 7- 11.

Where in your body are you carrying your feelings?

What is it you need in this moment . . . right now?

In Isaiah 55: 8-9 we read, "For my thoughts are not your thoughts, nor are your ways my ways, says the Lord. For as the heavens are higher than the earth, so are my ways higher than your ways and my thoughts than your thoughts." Ask the Lord to help you get understanding as you get quiet and answer the following questions:

1. If you had your way how would your situation be different?

2. How has God's way caused you pain and confusion?

3. If God is not the author of confusion, how do you reconcile the difference?

4. Is there "a hole" in your bucket? In other words, is there any past pain that continues to hinder you?

5. What are the messages that you battle?

Read James 1: 2-4; Romans 5: 3-4; and 1 Peter 1: 6-7

6. Are you able to embrace these messages? Explain.

7. What is it like to know that God uses trials to refine our character and make us useful to Him?

8. Do you think that everyone who struggles develops in this way? Why or why not?

Chapter 3
The Inner Lens

"My son is a darling to the whole world . . . except me. Rejection is subtle but piercing."

-Michelle, G.

"Let the redeemed of the Lord tell their story"
(Psalm 107:1, NIV)

View from Here

Everyone has a life story, and everyone's life story matters. For some of us, the journey has been hard and there is much to tell. Sadly, the overarching message of life's journey is often distorted. Words of defeat, rejection, and criticism have been downloaded into our hearts and minds in place of victory, acceptance, and truth. These messages that form our inner lens, can ultimately distort our image of our true self, God, and the world around us. While it's easy to see how this distortion has happened in our children's hearts, we may not realize the extent to which it has happened in our own heart as well.

It is this inner lens that shapes the core belief of an individual, dictating how that person sees the world and their place in it. How I wish we could easily repair this distorted inner vision with glasses! Yet, glasses are temporary, and only useful if the user decides to take care of them. My youngest child has glasses, yet tends to leave them anywhere we go: the beach, the playground, our tree house. She has proven that when a person is given something outside themselves to change their vision, it is a temporal and fragile tool. Our goal as parents and caregivers is to recognize the impact our stories have had on our own inner lens, and pursue change within ourselves so we can impact change within our children. Like Lasik surgery, we want to change our inner lens in a way that will be permanent, restoring true vision that is automatic and readily available, dependable, and true.

Attachment

I believe, like most children's therapists, that a person's inner lens is formed through a process called attachment during the early years of development. Attachment is the result of a process building the reciprocal relationship between caregiver and child. It is the primary intimate relationship, providing that child with a template for future intimate relationships, emotional competence, and their primary core beliefs or 'inner lens.' John Bowlby, the father of Attachment Theory, believed the process of attachment happens through the Cycle of Needs. This cycle is applicable for children in any culture across the world. It is a child's first impression of the world, and the nature of how this cycle is completed becomes the building block for all future interactions that child has.

Trust is Impacted 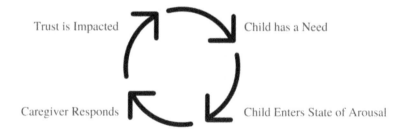 Child has a Need

Caregiver Responds   Child Enters State of Arousal

In this ideal model of a healthy family system, a child's needs are met again and again with love and affection by his or her caregiver. Trust and intimacy are established. The child in this scenario learns they are safe, loved, and nurtured, teaching them healthy cause and effect thinking. They begin to trust the world is a safe and predictable place, in which they have some power to make sure their needs are met. As children who experience this healthy cycle mature, it is my theory that they will ultimately view God as a loving and compassionate provider.

As we all know though, not every child is born into a healthy family system. In fact, relatively few are. When this Cycle of Needs is met with resentment and anger, and/or abusive caregiving, things turn out quite differently. A child in this cycle draws a distorted conclusion about themselves and the world. Their cause and effect thinking becomes skewed. Their core belief often becomes, "The world is scary but I have the power to provoke." These children often only feel connected with others when they are pushing buttons – it's the only way they have learned to relate. Their coping mechanisms are maladaptive and harmful to themselves and to their future relationships. I believe they come to view parents and God as vengeful scorekeepers, who demand nothing short of perfection.

A third scenario is the Cycle of Needs remaining unmet due to neglect, as in the case of disengaged parents, parents with addictions, or crowded orphanages. The natural conclusion a child draws in this situation, about the world and oneself is very sad. I will never forget an experience I had at a Bulgarian orphanage. Despite being filled to capacity with dozens of babies and toddlers in their cribs, the rooms were hauntingly silent. The children had learned not to even bother crying as it never helped their needs get met. Some were lying motionless while others rocked back and forth in their beds. It was a horrific sight. I found myself face-to-face with a little curly-haired boy who looked through me with his huge brown eyes. I tried engaging him with my eyes and voice, but he just stared back with a blank expression, as if catatonic. Gently touching him, I felt helpless as he remained frozen like a stone. The experience of neglect such as this, points kids to a belief system that says, "The world is unsafe and I have no power or value." Like the children in that orphanage, kids who download this message cope by self-soothing or shutting down. They arrive at the final conclusion that the only one they can trust to meet their needs is themselves. Parents and God are viewed as distant and disinterested, void of power or concern. Ultimately, they learn to engage in the world purely for their own purposes. Even when placed in loving homes, there is usually resistance to trust caregivers.

Other factors in addition to how a child's Cycle of Needs is met (or not met)

There are many other early influencers with the potential to injure a child's ability to attach. While early scenarios or patterns of care certainly lead to different styles of attachment, there are additional factors that can hinder a child's healthy attachment style. Even when a child's needs have been met with a loving parent, these additional factors create a barrier to the parent child bond. Some of these factors include:

- The birth mom's emotional state throughout pregnancy

- Pre-natal care (lack of nutrition, use of drugs, alcohol or tobacco)

- Pre-mature delivery

- Early Hospitalization

- Child's personality and genetic predisposition

- Trauma in Infancy or Early Development

- Loss of Attachment Figure (Birth parent, Caregiver, etc,)

- Developmental Delays or Challenges

- Illness &/or Special Needs

- Parenting techniques not conductive to attachment

- Resistance of parents to assist a child in recovery

Now I know you may be thinking of your child or children right now, but I want you to stop and think of your own childhood. Was there anything about your early life that left your 'inner working model' or core beliefs about yourself and your place in the world, vulnerable to false beliefs?

Some signs of unhealthy attachment in a child include:

- Resistance to parental love and affection (arches back, looks away, doesn't cuddle)

- Doesn't mimic affect (does not smile back, fails to reflect your expression)

- Fights being held (awkward to hold, rolls out of your arms etc.)

- Indiscriminately affectionate (happily shows affection to strangers or others)

- Lack of eye contact (looks down or away)

- Anxiousness (nervous behavior, nail biting, paces, rocks)

- Lying (even when it's obvious or not important)

- Hoarding food (over-eating, taking food in a sneaky way, storing food in pockets, room etc.)

- Poor peer relationships (difficulty making friends, lack of empathy, manipulative)

- Self-soothing behavior (rocking, head banging, thumb sucking, bed wetting)

- Controlling behavior (need to be in charge, use of sarcasm, manipulative)

When you think about the child or children you are raising, do any of these signs describe them? If so, ponder how that behavior might trigger you in light of your own childhood experiences.

In answer to these challenges, we must choose to answer our children's needs with what I call the 10-S strategy. Practiced consistently, this approach is a way we can begin to build trust and provide the right environment for our children to learn healthy attachment.

This 10-S strategy includes:

- Soft eyes (projecting love and not anger)

- Subtle touch (gentle hand on shoulder or back to encourage)

- Squeeze please (deep pressured squeeze type hugs)

- Sweet sound/voice (calm and soothing)

- Soothing smell (reminds them of home and mom-vanilla or lavender lotions, candles)

- Sustaining food (healthy, low sugar, protein)

- Sensory-rich experiences (play that involves the senses, example: sand tray, blowing bubbles)

- Structured nurturance (predictable routine that is loving . . . cuddle time with books before bed)

- Substitute/Replacement experiences (nurture that is focused on attachment and not age – i.e., rocking your 6 year old)

- Safe discipline (discipline protecting the child/caregiver relationship and strengthening the child's core beliefs)

A Parent's Battle

For additional resources on the subject of attachment strategies, I would direct you to other books and resources lists. The message of this book is less about what to do, and more about finding the motivation and strength to do it. It is no small task as a parent to consistently provide our children with each element of the 10-S strategy. We must begin by taking our own attachment history into consideration, recognizing whether or not we are able to act in love and freedom toward our children, or have we adapted to other ways of coping? On top of that, as parents we must be willing and able to submit our natural reactions as humans to what we know will benefit our child most. In other words, there are times we have to consciously override our own will and histories, choosing to do what feels most unnatural in order to give our children their best chance at healing.

For example, let's use one of the 10-S's: "Soft eyes." The eyes have often been called the "window to the soul," and yet how many times do we as parents fail when we choose to redirect our children with angry eyes? Instead of anger and frustration, our eyes must relay a message of love and trust. Another part of the 10-S strategy, "Sweet voice," is equally important. As you well know, keeping our voice sweet so it encourages a teachable moment, requires a great deal of self-control on our part. How often do we intend to teach, but end up scolding in anger? For our kids to reach wholeness and healing, they require more of us. However, faced with the challenge of rising to the occasion, it can seem an impossible task; and it would be, but for the grace of God coming to equip us and empower us, as we allow Him to heal the brokenness in our own hearts. When we can be 'wholehearted' our ability to override our natural reactions with purposed loving responses is greatly enhanced.

Our kids need us to grow in God, seeking His ways instead of ours. We must be willing to admit when we've failed, and then be ready to re-engage and try again. If our goal is facilitating a lasting change in our children, we have to see a lasting change made in us first. The struggle comes in the reality that we can't hit "pause" on our children's journey, while we take a break to get our own issues worked out first. It's up to us to learn how to do both at the same time. This job of providing parenting that heals, while simultaneously working on our own pain, is not for the faint of heart! It is for the humble and steadfast – albeit stubborn – warrior who believes they are capable of changing the world by engaging in the process of change themselves. I know how hard this journey is, and I know how incredibly overwhelming it feels, but do not fear! Our good God has given us all we need to see this thing through. We can draw from Him because He is good and gracious to His children. "To all who mourn in Israel, he will give a crown of beauty for ashes, a joyous blessing instead of mourning, festive praise instead of despair. In their righteousness, they will be like great oaks that the Lord has planted for his own glory." (Isaiah 61:3, NLT) Change begins the moment we begin to have hope, and believe change is possible for us, and for our children. Sometimes, securing the change begins by speaking out the truth in faith, regardless of whether we feel it yet or not. We read, "The tongue can bring death or life; those who love to talk will reap the consequences." (Proverbs 18:21, NLT) Through our words and actions, our goal is to confidently impart a message to our kids that says, "You belong to God. You are treasured and loved by a family. You are a journey-maker, and your outcome will be a good one because your future is full of promise and hope! I will never ever give up on you." The longer we stand firm in this belief, the more we will begin to see changes happen in ourselves and in our children.

Here are some behavioral signs you can look for, to know your children are healing and developing secure attachment:

- Establish and hold long lasting eye contact

- Show signs of reciprocal response (mirrors your facial expression, vocal tone)

- Seek comfort from their primary caregiver (chooses parent over others)

- Touch their caregiver gently

- Find their voice and ask for needs to be met

- Follow directions of their caregiver, even when they don't want to do so

- Show empathy

- Accept and offer love

- Glow with confidence (showing they believe they are genuinely loved and worthy of affection)

Now, let's look at them again from a perspective of your attachment healing with God.

- Establish and hold long lasting eye contact - do you seek His Face? His intimacy?

- Show signs of reciprocal response - do you know He delights in you? Do you respond to Him?

- Seek comfort from their primary caregiver – do you go to Him first for comfort over food, alcohol, caffeine or friends?

- Touch their caregiver gently – do you go to Him in quietness and trust?

- Find their voice and ask for needs to be met – do you call on the promises of God?

- Follow directions of their caregiver, even when they don't want to do so – do you listen & obey?

- Show empathy – do you show compassion for self and others from God's perspective?

- Accept and offer love – are you able to receive and give love freely?

- Glow with confidence (showing they believe they are genuinely loved and worthy of affection)

We know we are healing, the more we begin to resemble our Savior in our words and actions. The path to wholeness is marked by our declarations, the fruit of our lives, and the vision we have aligning in our daily walk. Seeing these areas progress gives us hope we are being changed day by day into His image and likeness. Our reflection comes clearly into view the more we begin to resemble Him. "And the Lord—who is the Spirit— makes us more and more like him as we are changed into his glorious image." (2 Corinthians 3:18, NLT) It's a lifelong process, and it isn't a destination we will fully arrive at this side of heaven. However, we can choose to move closer, and become more like our heavenly Father through our choices and daily practices.

Delay is Not Denial

I love the saying, "Never doubt in the dark what God has shown you in the light." When darkness has prevailed for so long in our life and circumstances, we so effortlessly forget His promises. The silence of heaven can cause us to start second-guessing ourselves, wondering why God hasn't answered our prayers, or worse, if He has denied them.

Mistakenly projecting the experiences we had with our own parents on God, often means we are projecting false beliefs that can leave us spinning in confusion. For example, if we had a parent who was aloof and distant, it is only natural that we assume our heavenly Father is the same. God's desire is for our relationship with Him to always be moving forward into deeper levels of trust and love. As we have all experienced, it takes a certain level of resistance for growth to happen. Like a parent who runs next to a child learning how to ride a bike, sometimes He allows us to feel alone for a moment. Of course, He is always right there, by our side ready to catch us. He wants us to learn how to trust His presence and His nearness, even when we can't see or feel Him close. Too often we pass our hurts up to God like we're playing a game of Hot Potato, never really looking at what we're giving Him. We've got to stop! We need to know our false beliefs and past hurts well for two reasons: so they won't ensnare us again, and so we can give God full glory for healing them.

Awareness of our pain and false projections allow us to become honest about our need for something different. We can ask God to reveal the truth about His character and love for us instead of the lies we've bought into. This journey will require relentless persistence on our part, bringing to Him all of who we are. Every piece of our past, present, and future belong in His hands. We need not fear His reaction. As my Pastor once reminded me, "We are not equal to our destiny, but Jesus is." He will help us, and guide us to recognize our false beliefs if we allow Him.

You can begin by being self-aware of what you are feeling. Label your feeling, and recognize where you hold it in your body. Where are you experiencing shame, anger, loneliness etc.? When have you felt this way before? Ask yourself when you first experienced this emotion, and what was happening at that time. I'll share a personal example . . . I've already laid so much out there, why not? I can't remember all the details, but my spouse had disappointed me. I felt unheard and uncared for, though I can't remember what on earth he had said or done. It involved needing him to care for me, and his unwillingness to do so.

I think there may have been a basketball game on. I recognized that my reaction was a bit out of balance with the situation. For some reason I was feeling deep rejection and sadness . . . and panic. I hid myself in my bathroom and began to ask God to reveal what was going on with me at a deeper level. Instead of focusing on someone else's behavior, I asked God to show me what nerve it was hitting, and to heal that place. I asked myself a series of questions such as those listed above. I remembered feeling the same way when I lost my course schedule in college because my parents were arguing over whose turn it was to help with tuition. It had been a cycle for me as a child of divorce and remarriage. I always heard about how my mother should have paid for braces, how my father didn't pay for camp, child support and on and on.

God showed me that at a very deep level I held a false belief based on experience. I heard myself say, "Why am I a pain in the ass to everyone who is supposed to care for me?" And there it was . . . a long held belief that I was somehow 'unworthy' of love and help. Even as I write this, there is a tinge of pain in my heart. It was the lie that led to other lies, about taking care of myself, and never needing anyone. It led to performance and perfectionism, and an ever-pressing sense of what others thought of me. Even now, I wonder what you may be thinking since I used the word 'ass.' Yet, as God revealed the lie, He also reminded me of the truth: He loves me and longs to care for me at a moment's notice. I am not perfect, and I don't need to be.

He loves me as I am. He is never distant or too busy to meet with me, and He is surely enough. He is an able, and willing Father and partner. Too often I had been aware of the truth, but unaware of where I needed to apply it. It doesn't make a difference if you have the sharpest weapon, if the target is obscure. Things would be different now for me, as I was armed with not only the truth, but also the knowledge of the lie.

Chapter 3 Study

The Inner Lens

Now that we've examined where you are, let's look at where you've been.

"And we, who with unveiled faces all reflect the Lord's glory, are being transformed into His likeness with ever-increasing glory" (2 Corinthians 3:17, NLT)

1. Finish these sentences from your own childhood (age 0-8) perspective:

My world feels_____

_____

I can count on_____

_____

I trust_____

_____

My future is_____

_____

Now repeat these questions from your adult mindset. Are there differences? What about your child's perspective given their early beginnings?

2. Explain how this "Inner Lens" might be acted upon in everyday life. How might it cause difficulty to your parent-child relationship? What about the parent-child relationship between you and God the Father?

In Isaiah 42:16 we read, "I will lead the blind by a road they do not know, by paths they have not known I will guide them. I will turn the darkness before them into light, the rough places into level ground. These are the things I will do, and I will not forsake them."

3. Do you consider your present walk a circumstance in which you feel blind? In what ways?

4. Are you able to trust God to lead you? Do you feel you have a secure attachment with Him to do so?

5. Read Psalm 119:105. In reference to the previous question, how can you apply this and the Isaiah passage to your life?

6. What do you think are the promises God has made to those who suffer? Write out Romans 5: 3-5; Psalm 30: 5, 11, Jeremiah 31:13. Will you choose to believe these promises personally? Write out your statements of faith to the Lord. What are you willing to give to Him now?

Take a moment to reflect on any new insight that has been revealed to you throughout this homework. Pray that God might guide you so that you may see the truth that is before you. Ask that He strengthen you along this path of revelation.

Chapter 4

Heart & Soul

"There was a day I lost it. I scared my 10 year old child with my anger. She responded with terrified screams, wailing under her bed for a birth mom she hadn't known since she was two."

-Liz, H.

"I fell in love with you heart and soul."

Heart and Soul

I love the phrase "heart and soul." It describes something with wholeness, something completely in alignment and agreement. We want "heart and soul" healing to describe the work we do in ourselves as parents, and that we hope to see in our children. Before we can change our inner model, we have to first become aware of our false beliefs. Through the varied experiences we have in life, our brains have come to hold certain conclusions we cling to at the very center of who we are. These core beliefs, which are often subconscious and unarticulated, drive our stated beliefs, thoughts, feelings, and ultimately our behaviors. In order to remain in control of these things, we must constantly check to make sure we are in alignment with the core beliefs we choose to have, rather than the ones we default to, based on life experiences.

Lotus flowers offer a beautiful example of how we are to navigate the often-murky waters of choosing our beliefs. Normally found in the muddy waters of lakes and ponds, the lotus reveals its lovely flower only by the light of day. At night, its head closes up and goes beneath the water, only to resurface again in the morning. Like the lotus flower, our desire is to remain in the light, pressing through our gloomy circumstances, to bloom again in the morning after the night. However, we can only do this so long as we remain rooted in the soil of truth, stretching for the light. By taking every thought and lie captive, we strengthen our ability to reemerge in full bloom above our circumstances.

You may be wondering, "How do I become grounded and rooted in truth? What is truth?" That's a big question to ask, but before you panic, let me assure you the answer is simple. I am no great philosopher, willing to spend endless amounts of time trying to define truth. I only ask the question to make this point: all human truth is objective and defined by perspective. The only real truth is found in Jesus who said "I am the way, the truth, and the life. No one can come to the Father except through me." (John 14:6, NLT). As believers in Christ, we define truth in Him. By implication, this means the truth of our life stories must also be defined in Him. When we get a vision for our life that is grounded in the truth of Christ, our life will blossom. Only then can we offer parenting that heals a child's heart and soul. That is what restorative parenting looks like, parenting that heals in the most essential parts of a child's life. It's parenting that believes a child's inner lens can be changed to see themselves and the world the way Christ does. It is parenting that moves with complete faith that a child's story can be completely redeemed, and their future secured. Parents who engage in this type of parenting have a profound conviction springing up from a deep place of experiencing healing themselves.

Opposition

One barrier that is commonly combating our faith today, has been created by the lies of, what I call, the 'Inner Orphan Spirit.' You do not have to have the history of actually being an orphan to feel the weight of it. The Inner Orphan can be embraced through doors left open by neglect, parental apathy, early trauma, and loss. Many adults I encounter carry this mindset with them, even though they may not realize it. The 'Orphan Mindset' whispers lies in their ear saying, "You are not worth remembering. You're forgotten. No one cares. You must take care of yourself. To get it done right, you have to do it yourself. Pull yourself up by your bootstraps and press on. Strive. Try. Work harder. You don't need anyone, and they don't want you." I think women are particularly vulnerable to this mindset as there are so many supports in our culture to support it. We feel the pressure to be smartest, prettiest, richest, thinnest, youngest, and the list goes on. We hold the belief that if we are not the "est" we are failures.

The Orphan Mindset entertains a spirit of rejection, which like a swinging door, leaves one feeling both rejected, and also wanting to reject. Twin to rejection is a spirit of rebellion, which prompts one to shut others out and do things their own way. The M.O. of the Inner Orphan is to pull from our past experiences, flashing images from our history and promoting feelings of desperate longing and loneliness. It fills our head with echoing voices of defeat and despair, prompting us to build impenetrable walls of isolation. The Orphan Spirit is relentless. Its goal is to disconnect you from love, purposing to devastate you, and leave you feeling utterly unworthy of care and concern. When the Orphan Spirit has done its work, it is nearly impossible to fathom a God who sees you and loves you immeasurably. And when love cannot find a way into a heart, there is little chance sincere love will find a way out. As we have all experienced, it is a lot of work to give what you don't have.

If you don't have an overflow of love to give, it's ultimately exhausting and unsatisfying to even try. Yet failure only resurrects old battles against the lies that you are worthless, and need to try harder and be better. This vicious cycle keeps us trapped, feeling driven to keep striving, yet leaves us without the resources to succeed. This is what parenting out of our own Orphan Spirit looks like: endless work, no satisfaction, and no peace. When we are battling our own Orphan Spirit, we parent brokenly, with an attitude of performance that drives us to rescue other orphans and work, work, work. If we really look at ourselves honestly, it's driving us to try and perform for God, rather than pursue a relationship with Him. As long as we keep the Orphan Spirit alive and well in our lives, we will not experience healing and wholeness in our own hearts, let alone see healing come to our children.

Being overcome with battling thoughts and habits of rejection, self-preservation, and striving in our own strength, do not lead to healthy attachment and healing. If the Orphan Spirit can sink its hooks into a parent and child in the same household, its efforts are mysteriously multiplied. Like two porcupines trying to dance, the relationship is painfully hard, and the results are often disastrous. Until we know and embrace the good promises God has for us, and fully find our identity in His freedom and grace, parenting to restore and heal will always be a difficult task. You might be an expert on all the best parenting methods and techniques, but without genuine love and grace overflowing from your life, that knowledge alone won't get you anywhere. I really don't have to tell you that though – you've probably already experienced it for yourself, and are now asking the question, "So how do I get there?"

First, you must realize there is no place of "arriving" in this journey. There is only the daily choice to live and parent wholeheartedly as a way of life. Parenting with heart and soul requires living freely with heart and soul. Our ability to live wholeheartedly is rooted in how well we know our identity in Christ. While we all "know" who we are in Christ, truly recognizing and claiming your identity in the light of God takes intentionality and mindful intention.

My friend, Dr. Ron Waggoner, developed a theory he calls, "Spirit Managed Thinking." Understanding this theory has to start by understanding a little about the brain. I am not a neurologist, but from the little I know about the undeniable and fascinating complexities of our brains, it leaves me in awe of how amazing God is! Dr. Waggoner states the brain holds a person's collection of memories and past experiences, which together continually condition how the brain reacts to present experiences and accomplishes the "living of life." For example, when I smell lilacs I am immediately taken back to my Grandparents' farm; good emotions are evoked, and I feel a sense of joy. On the other hand, any time I see a German Shepherd my heart begins to race and I freeze with wide-eyed fear. When I think about this reaction I remember films of Nazi Germany that I was shown as a youth growing up in a Jewish family. These films were shown to my youth group and were unedited and horrific. I empathized so much with the victims that I grew terrified of the German Shepherd dogs that were used to rally them like cattle. The point is, the brain is a powerful record keeper, providing us with information in the present, based on experiences in the past. Sometimes these experiences aren't even ours, but we have inherited their conclusions none-the-less. Often our parents will hand down their conclusions to us as children. For example, one of my parents lost his brother to drowning, while swimming with friends in the river. Though he always made sure we loved the water and knew how to swim, I have always been afraid of the unpredictable nature of the river. I never go swimming in something I can't see the bottom of clearly, and I have passed that conclusion/fear onto my own children.

You might already be thinking of your own 'conclusions' and may recognize that there are many sources of our belief systems, and those of our children. We might begin to understand how a child who spends their formative years lacking love and nurturing, is likely to see the world as a cold and unfeeling place. When that child has grown up unable to trust, their brain becomes programmed to respond from an internal view of defensiveness or despair. A brain working from past perspectives instead of today's truths, will find it very difficult to respond with reason and trust.

"Reprogramming" our brain's responses can be difficult, but not impossible. The brain is like a King trying to rule and reign over our life. The good news is that while we might not be able to change how that "king" behaves, we can choose to dethrone and overrule him!

Referring back to Dr. Waggoner's theory of "Spirit Managed Thinking" we can be assured that we are more than our brain. I will let him have the pleasure of explaining this theory in detail in his own book, *Living Confidently Out of your Mind*, but for the purpose of this book, I want to share some key elements that we can hang onto as we move forward. According to Waggoner, as part of our body, our brain also dies with our body. Because it remains with our physical body after death, it cannot be accountable before God. The implication is our spirit-self is separate from our brain.   Recognizing   we   are something apart from our brain is crucial to enjoying our faith and preparing us for accountability before God. Waggoner concludes, "We are spirits in charge of a body, not a body in charge of a spirit." By adopting this theory, we can hope to parent from "Spirit Managed Thinking" instead of remaining enslaved to our natural responses.

"Therefore, dear brothers and sisters, you have no obligation to do what your sinful nature urges you to do. For if you live by its dictates, you will die. But if through the power of the Spirit you put to death the deeds of your sinful nature, you will live. 14 For all who are led by the Spirit of God are children of God. So you have not received a spirit that makes you fearful slaves. Instead, you received God's Spirit when he adopted you as his own children. Now we call him, 'Abba, Father.'" (Romans 8:12-15, NLT)

Who's the Boss?

So if we dethrone the brain, who's in charge? Remember that great little sitcom, *Who's the Boss?* The irony of it was that no one was really sure if it was Angela, the homeowner, or Tony the housekeeper. A flirtatious little 30 minute show was silly and fun to watch. Unfortunately, when we are unsure of who's in charge, the results are much less entertaining. We can find ourselves being pulled, with some force I might add, in several directions.

As people, we are fearfully and wonderfully made with complexities and incredible struggles between three parts of self: body, soul, and spirit. Today there is a lot of talk about the soul and its care. We have 'soul care' programs at church and in our communities. Oprah even has a designated 'Soul Care' programming schedule. The words are thrown around a lot. There are a lot of wonderful people doing wonderful things to help us feel good in our soul. How many of us really even know how to define our soul though? It is a bit confusing, isn't it? We hear ways to get more from our brain, beware of our flesh, listen to our gut, go with our heart . . . and the list goes on. Here is how I boil it down: We are like a train with three compartments, all with the ability to move, but not all with the capacity to lead well.

If we were to unpack each of these compartments, we might argue the following: Body (brain & all physical processes) Soul (heart, gut, personality) Spirit (our divine essence.) We were designed to be Spirit led, though it battles for control with our Soul and Body, in a world that pulls for our attention in their directions. Living in a way that honors the hierarchy of the Spirit, Spirit Managed Living is how we bring our best to our children. It keeps us grounded in the truth of who we are, and keeps us focused on what we are called to accomplish in this world: to love God, ourselves, and others. It is the daily process of putting on our oxygen mask first, so we can then help our children learn to access that same grace they need and deserve to thrive. Choosing to live this way is an intentional battle stance, forcing us to pause and make all our actions and thoughts deliberate and grounded in truth.

In *Man's Search for Meaning*, Victor Frankl noted: "Between stimulus and response, there is a space. In that space is our power to choose our response. In our response lies our growth and our freedom." Spirit Managed Living takes advantage of that space, so we can parent intentionally and proactively, bringing healing, growth, and freedom for our children and ourselves.

Chapter 4 Study

Heart & Soul

"If we live by the Spirit, let us also be guided by the Spirit." (Galatians 5:25, NLT) We have been called to abundant life. Yet, this abundance includes trials and trouble. Our Savior willingly accepted His assignment for suffering out of His great love for us. As we continue in our study, we will seek to understand what this gift means to us as we receive it. As you begin, pray that the Lord will reveal your true identity in Him, giving you greater understanding of the life He has called you to live.

In John 3:3 Jesus says, "I tell you the truth, no one can see the kingdom of God unless he is born again."

1. Jesus is talking about a spiritual rebirth as we place our trust in Him. Do you remember this birth in your own life? What was born in you?

2. What had to die in your life in order that you be made new? What needs to die still?

3. Do you find it difficult at times to yield to this new life rather than your old one? Explain.

Our greatest contentment in life comes when Christ increases in us, yet in order for this to happen we must decrease. As we look at the process of yielding read John 3:22-30.

4. What did it take for John to yield to Christ?

5. How are you challenged by this example?

6. Do you think you act in your own power and strength when yielding? (Write out Philippians 2:13)

7. Name 3 descriptive qualities that you wish to develop more consistently. Use these as considerations when you hit 'pause' before responding, as you interact with others. For example your 'Self Talk' may sound like this: "I am loving, poised, and confident. My reaction will match those qualities."

Find 3 scripture verses to help train your mind to grasp this image. Those without a vision perish - so get a vision of who you want to be! My vision for myself includes these 3 qualities:

_____,

_____,

and_____.

Supportive Scripture Includes:

My Self-Talk Includes:

Chapter 5

Party Pooper

"There were nights when I cried myself to sleep, mornings when I shuddered to wake and start my day."

-Naomi, F.

"Every party has a pooper"

My mother used to sing the "Party Pooper" song when one of us was in a bad mood and didn't want to join in the fun. It's a spoof of the 1916 song *Pretty Baby* by Gus Kahn, Tony Jackson, and Egbert Van Alstyne. The lyrics of the original are, "Everybody loves a baby, that's why I'm in love with you, pretty baby, pretty baby." But you may remember it best from the movie Father of the Bride, when Franc the wedding coordinator sang the Party Pooper version.

Let me remind you, in a friendly way, we have an unwanted and uninvited guest at the party of our lives – and he's a lot worse than a tight-fisted father of the bride. Remember, the process of healing ourselves and our kids will bring a very real supernatural battle right to our doorstep. We have a real enemy who loves nothing more than causing pain early in a person's life, so he can cause them a lifetime of brokenness and lies. We must choose to fight with discernment and tenacity, ever watchful of what we allow in our experience of life. Our "party pooper" comes to steal, kill, and destroy every part of joy in our lives. While our enemy is crouching at our door like a raging lion, we need only remember this: we already have complete victory and freedom in Christ Jesus. When we make the decision to shape our identity in light of our victorious position in Christ, especially as parents, our enemy dispatches a host of adversaries to assail our lives. If we were to take a roll call, I am convinced it would include fear, resentment, guilt and shame, weariness, and others sent to undermine and totally destroy us. As we learn Spirit

Managed Living, it's time we recognize these adversaries so we can stop them in their tracks.

Fear

Fear is first in line, waiting and ready to make trouble, even as the ink is drying on the adoption application. Fear attempts to corrode our faith, by attacking where we are most vulnerable. Fear whispers, "This will never work. You won't have enough money. What will others say?" Fear's favorite line of all though, is the infamous "What if?" This is the phrase fear will lead with nine times out of ten. "What if something happens to you when you're traveling? What if your children don't like you? What if the judge says 'no'? What if the child has AIDS?" The speculation goes on and on. Even years after you've come home, Fear still tries to speak into your parenting by introducing new "what if's" and nudging you to invite his pal Worry to join the party. Like Fear, Worry asks questions too: "Shouldn't you be concerned . . . ?" There are a million ways you might finish that sentence: ". . . that she may never be accepted by her peers?" or ". . . your child will resent you?" or ". . . that something might happen?"

Of course, Fear and Worry are nasty liars. They want you to invite them in, so you can later entertain their friends, Dread and Panic. Together, this terrible foursome love watching parents shut down and become frozen, convinced they are completely powerless. Fear has a big mouth, and it loves to keep moving. There's an old saying that says to never let a salesman beyond your gate. If he gets beyond your gate, he's on your porch. If you let him on the porch, he's in your house. If you let him in the house, you'll never get him out until you buy what he's selling. Just like a salesman, Fear has a lot to sell and you would do best to not be buying! Fear brings a whole host of other problems with it. Like a cockroach, fear multiplies easily and spreads its nastiness wildly.

Resentment

Resentment is a clever adversary, sneaky and judgmental. Resentment slips in unnoticed and begins influencing our mind, molding our thoughts to blame others for our problems. Painting rosy pictures of the past, resentment twists our perspective by causing us to think, "Things were better then." Another method resentment uses is giving us a distorted lens to see others, giving us the impression "things are better there for them." By using the phrases "would have," "should have," and "could have," resentment, if unchecked, can have you questioning almost every decision you've ever made. Resentment's goal is division, especially between you and your spouse. It will taunt you saying, "She did this; it was her idea." or "He should have known better and stopped this; if he had, we wouldn't be in this mess." Resentment causes you to waste emotion by dwelling on the "if only's" of your situation. Like Fear, Resentment has a few friends it wants to introduce you to as well. Two that Resentment is very close with are Unforgiveness and Bitterness. They show up when you are unaware, and love to return over and over again, even after you've sincerely tried to throw them out. Like lice, they are hard to see, and difficult to get rid of. Just when you think you've conquered Resentment's ploy to blame others, it will turn the tables and push you to disdain yourself. Once you've accepted this level of resentment, it will pull out the big guns and entice you to resent God. The roots of Resentment, Unforgiveness, and Bitterness go down deep in your heart, and it can take a lot of digging to be rid of them once and for all. Resentment is a bully, and close behind it ready to torment you come Guilt and Shame.

Guilt and Shame

Like a conjoined monster, Guilt and Shame go everywhere together. Guilt consistently speaks condemnation, and Shame encourages you to isolate yourself. They tag- team their efforts with a goal of making you feel worthless and degraded, setting you up to embrace one of their successors, Anger or Despair. Guilt and Shame also partner with Fear, compounding your feelings of isolation by making you afraid to let others know how you really think, feel, and behave. They heap on the condemnation to keep you alone and vulnerable.

This terrible duo has been collaborating forever; they've been working on their act since the Garden and are very good at what they do. Ultimately, their goal is to separate you from the truth, from support, and from God. Using images of poverty and orphans, they manipulate adoptive parents into thinking they will "ruin it" for others if they admit how real their struggles are. Of course, Guilt and Shame know how to beat up on parents in any situation with messages of self-condemnation and embarrassment, but they are especially adept at attacking adoptive parents. Cousins of Guilt and Shame, Vanity and Pride often come to visit and can become formidable foes to defeat. Like mice, this family group never comes alone and leaves destruction wherever they go.

Weariness

You've been there. You've heard the tempting voice of Weariness whisper in your ear, "You're tired. You've worked at this long enough – it's okay to quit!" It sounds like sweet relief, but Weariness is always a precursor to Despair and Depression. It lays the groundwork for Despair and Depression to build on, almost before you realize what's happening. Like a heavy wet wool blanket, Weariness attempts to cover you and bring you down. Forming a strategic partnership with Chaos, Confusion, and Gluttony, Weariness works tirelessly to drag you down mentally, physically, emotionally, and spiritually. Beware of Weariness. It will come in the night causing you to wake up more tired than when you went to bed. Worry is often found in the company of Weariness; they go hand in hand, and are on a rampage to steal all your joy, peace, and contentment. Their tactics are designed to render you ineffective and hopeless. The day you quit, stay down for the count, and give up the fight, is the day they have accomplished their goal. You cannot surrender to them even an inch of your ground, or else they'll come barging in and take a mile. Once Weariness and Worry have a foothold in your life, you can be sure Stress and Anxiety will not be far behind. After that, you can almost rest assured Illness will come riding in with even more destruction.

Now what?

Of course, this list is not exhaustive. There are other people better suited to describe the adversaries you will face, but in my experience there seems to be a strategic and collaborative approach to the battle waged against us as parents. In response, we too must be strategic and deliberate. I trust you will find (and have already found) other books and workshops that will give you more specific information about your parenting approach and the needs of your child.

The purpose I want to accomplish in this book, is to equip you for the emotional and mindset battles you're fighting. Following recommendations, based not on research, or years of study, but rather on my own personal experiences and what has worked for me. I don't for a moment mean to imply I have it all together, or have in any way "arrived." I have seen a lot of adversity though, and have begun to notice patterns in the midst of it all. That's what I share with you – a strategy from one who has fought the battle you're in, and is still fighting today. My approach is simple, and very common sense. Sometimes when we are in the middle of a storm, common sense can be hard to find though. This is my fallback strategy, to resist the enemies sent to attack me.

Strategize

As I mentioned earlier, there is such value in using breath to hit 'reset' in our mind and body. Taking a deep inhale, and slow exhale can do wonders to slow a spinning mind and racing heart. I try to focus on nothing but breath for 5 minutes. If I'm really in a panic or find myself borrowing pain from the past, or fear of the future, I do my "list 3 of 3" routine. That is, I list three things I see, three things I hear, and three things I can touch in my surroundings. This practice helps bring me into the present and interrupts my wandering mind. My next line of questions to myself are these: "What am I feeling?" "Where in my body am I feeling it?" and "What is it I need?" I notice my body. Where am I holding tension? Is my breath still shallow, or can I do my '7-11'; inhale for 7 and exhale for 11? Are my jaws tight? Am I holding stress in my shoulders? I also try to take other factors into consideration that might be leaving me vulnerable, such as physical exhaustion, hunger, and dehydration. I then act on meeting my physical needs, if possible, as I practice taking care of myself. Usually that involves moving my body.

Next, I get quiet before the Lord and ask Him to reveal the truth of the situation. I ask for help in evaluating what belief system is at work in my heart. I want to identify the message that belief system is trying to instill in this moment. This will require that I get quiet, and be willing to be brutally honest. It may not be pretty, and it sure isn't where I want to stay, but I let it out. Journaling is helpful in this process for me, as well as art.

Red flags that go up if my thought life includes any of the following:

- I'm not good enough

- I need more

- I can do it myself

- I'll make it work

- No one really cares

- Life is so hard

- If only . . .

- I will always be . . .

- I am . . . (followed by anything negative)

Then ask the crucial question: is it based on current experience, or an earlier one? Where have you held this belief system before? When did this message first enter your framework? Is it a long held belief? What was happening? Who were the players involved in this portion of your story? This is not about assigning blame, but rather taking inventory of your inner tapes, and screening them for lies. Sometimes your circumstances will provide evidence that appear contrary to God's Word, and you will need to choose. That is, you will be in a position to make a choice between your inner beliefs and God's word. It is vital that you know the word of God, and have some scriptures memorized to be readily available in your arsenal. There may be circumstances when this process will be a quick one, and other times it may take days or weeks of reflection and discernment. The most crucial piece of advice is this: do not stop pursuing God's truth, and His involvement in your process of living freely.

Certainly, our feelings are never to be trusted as evidence of truth. Instead, welcome Faith into your situation. Equipped with Faith, you can choose wisely what you will believe. When we partner with Faith, we will find

Hope is not far behind, and together they move our heart and mind closer to Resolve and Courage. This powerful foursome works together to strengthen you, helping you reach a point of releasing the truth and promises of God into your situation.

Now Release! You can do it in your mind, thinking it quietly, but I find it most effective when you engage your voice. There is something powerful about taking a stand in the spirit, by using words spoken out loud. Scripture tells us the tongue holds the power of life and death (Proverbs 18:21). That's a lot of potential power resting on the words we speak! It's time we choose to release life, by confessing life with our tongue. In practice, speak to things as they really are in the spiritual realm, not the way they appear in the physical, natural realm. For example, in the natural you may feel afraid, unworthy, and alone. You may be experiencing panic attacks, isolation from everyone around you, and desperation of the worst kind. This is your experience, but it is not your reality. Your reality is based on the truth seen in Scripture that says you are seated with Christ, you are full of peace, and surrounded by victory and love. Choose to see yourself through spiritual eyes; everything else is an illusion.

There's a scene from the movie Hook that I just love. Peter Banning is speaking to Granny Wendy, trying to make sense of the crisis of losing his children to Hook. This business man in crisis is standing with his hands on his hips, feet wide apart, when Granny Wendy reveals a picture of him in the same pose as Pan. She softly asks, "Peter, don't you know who you are?" Sometimes I imagine the Lord asking the same question of us: "Don't you know who you are?" We have been purchased at the highest price, bought and redeemed by the blood of Christ. We are now children of God, and are only seen by God as the righteousness of His Son. We have complete victory. All joy and peace are ours, yet we are faced with circumstances and memories the enemy would use to deceive us into forgetting. Like Peter Banning, we suit up with cell phone in hand, worry lines on our forehead, and fight our way through the day. We struggle through our circumstances forgetting all we need to do is remember who we are and soar!

Chapter 5 Study
Party Pooper

"The world and its desire are passing away, but those who do the will of God live forever." (1 John 1:17, NLT)

1. What have you been battling recently? What are the lies you've been fighting? Read Romans Chapter 8.

2. How is it that we are able to walk according to the Spirit and not the flesh? (See verses 3-5)

3. What hope do we have, if the body is dead because of sin? (See verse 10)

4. How is it that we are called 'children of God' and what does that mean for our lives? (See verses 14-17) How are you impacted by these verses?

5. How do you feel when you read that we suffer with Christ, so that we may also be glorified with Him?

6. What is the hope that Paul is referring to in verses 24-25?

7. Is it difficult to keep your focus here? What help do you have? (See verses 26-27)

8. Read the powerful words that finish this chapter (see verses 31-39). In what ways are you inspired? Are you able to receive the hope of this message? Explain.

True Reflection

Read the scripture of God's truths about who we are in Him as believers. Which ones are hard for you to believe for yourself? Spend time in prayerful meditation with the Lord, asking Him to help you download these truths, removing any unbelief. Consider which ones you would like to impart to your child through this healing process as well.

In Christ, I am:

Born Anew (1 Peter 1:23)

Forgiven (Ephesians 1:7, Hebrews 9:14, Colossians 1:14, 1 John 2:12, 1 John 1:9)

New Creation (2 Corinthians 5:17)

The Temple of the Holy Spirit (1 Corinthians 6:19)

 Delivered (Colossians 1:13)

Redeemed (1 Peter 1:18-19 Galatians 3:13)

A Saint (Romans 1:7, 1 Corinthians 1:2, Philippians 1:1)

Blessed (Deuteronomy 28:1-14, Galatians 3:9)

The Head and not the tail (Deuteronomy 20:13)

Holy (1 Peter 1:1, Ephesians 1:4)

Victorious (Revelation 21:7)

Set Free (John 8:31-33)

Strong in the Lord (Ephesians 6:10)

Joint heir with Christ (Romans 8:17)

Complete in Him (Colossians 2:10)

Crucified with Christ (Galatians 2:20)

Alive with Christ (Ephesians 2:5)

Reconciled to God (2 Corinthians 5:18)

Firmly rooted (Colossians 2:7)

The Righteousness of God (2 Corinthians 5:21, 1 Peter 2:24)

Healed (1 Peter 2:24, Isaiah 53:6)

Being changed into His image (2 Corinthians 3:18, Philippians 1:6)

Beloved of God (Colossians 3:12, Romans 1:7, 1 Thessalonians 1:4)

Established to the end (Colossians 1:8)

I am God's child (John 1:12, 1 John 3:1)

Friend of God (John 15:15)

I am united with the Lord, and I am one spirit with Him (1 Corinthians 6:17)

Temple of the Holy Spirit (1 Corinthians 6:19-20)

The Body of Christ (Corinthians 12:27)

I have direct access to the throne of grace through Christ (Hebrews 4:14-16)

Free from condemnation (Romans 8:1-2)

I am assured that God works for my good in all circumstances (Romans 8:28)

More than a Conqueror (Romans 8:31-39)

Secure and Protected (1 John 5:18)

I have been established, anointed and sealed by God (2 Corinthians 1:21-22)

I have a mind set on things above (Colossians 3:1-4)

I am hidden with Christ in God; Confident and Hopeful (Philippians 1:6)

A Citizen of Heaven (Philippians 3:20)

Have the Mind of Christ (1 Corinthians 2:16, Philippians 2:4-11)

Powerful, Loving, and with Sound Mind, I am a branch of Jesus Christ, the true vine, and a channel of His life (John 15:5)

Chosen to be Fruit bearing (John 15:16)

Have the Spirit of God within me (1 Corinthians 2:12-3:16)

Have an Inheritance with Christ (Ephesians 1:11)

I am a minister of reconciliation for God (Ephesians 2:6)

I am sealed with Christ (Ephesians 1:13)

I am Seated with Christ in the Heavenly Places (Ephesians 3:12)

I am a member of God's Household (Ephesians 2:19)

A Shining Star (Philippians 2:14-15)

Full of Peace, Joy, and Gentleness (Philippians 4:4-7)

I may approach God with freedom and confidence. Powerful (Philippians 4:13; Timothy 1:7)

"If we live by the Spirit, let us also be guided by the Spirit." (Galatians 5:25)

Chapter 6

You are What You Eat

"My heart knows I need you, but my mind screams for chocolate."

-Marcy, D.

"Chocolate is a food group"

Castles in the Sand

In time of frustration, I have said that raising my children has felt as futile as building sand castles close to the shoreline. Sometimes, it appeared that anything I had tried to build in them washed away with the tide. There have been days when I couldn't take it any longer and just checked out. I didn't really intend to, but I found myself lingering on facebook, eating sugar to find comfort, and spending crazy amounts of time avoiding my kids with busy work. It's not pretty to admit, but it's real. Sometimes I'm just plain tired. I've got nothing left, and will mentally count down the years we have left in the same home, in a crazy attempt to envision a life beyond the finish line. Then something worse happens . . . the 'what if' wheel begins to spin, and I imagine that the finish line will never come. What if my children never make progress? What if they will be stuck forever in second grade level? What if they lack the skills needed to be safe? Employed? Secure? This manifests into a full blown panic, and on empty I reach for the Nutella and the remote. It's a vicious cycle, and I can find myself spinning.

I'm sure you've heard the phrase, "You are what you eat." I believe this statement isn't limited to apply only to the food we put in our mouths, but the way we nourish each part of our person: body, soul, and spirit. If we choose practices that close us off to the journey of growth and awakening, we will miss the growth in store for us. How can we allow our spirit to conquer the battles of our mind, if we are sugared up and checked out? The health of all other areas of self are indications of what our spirit needs. As a general rule, when things are out of alignment in the physical and emotional parts of our lives, it's often a clue something is amiss in our spirit. While self-care in these areas is important, we must remember that the body and soul aren't meant to lead; they simply aren't built that way. To keep our body and soul from pulling us in directions we don't want to go, we need to pay close attention to what they are telling us.

Body

Our physical bodies have been designed to tell us what battle our spirit is in. If we are willing to quiet ourselves, pay attention, and listen to these messages, we will find our body can speak to us. Tense muscles, clinched fists and jaws all point to tension and stress. They say, "I'm holding on to more than I should; please talk to God and listen to your spirit." When your shoulders are so knotted and tight, they practically touch your ear lobes, it's time to take notice. Your body is screaming, "Hey! Take care of things!"

We can be guilty of abusing our body to block out mental and emotional stress. When we do this, we are essentially using our body as a shield to protect our feelings, literally letting our body take all the hits. This can look a variety of different ways. Trying to fuel our body on a steady diet of sugar and "comfort food" can be soothing, but does little to help our body recover from the circumstances surrounding us. On the other end of the spectrum, extreme obsession with dieting and exercise can be another guise of abusing our body, as a way to cope with our inner emotional pain. The point isn't what we do or don't do to our body, but rather that we learn to treat our bodies in a healthy, balanced way.

There came a time in my life that I had to realize that several years of facing the storms of our family had taken a toll on my physical health. I was having trouble sleeping, yet was tired all the time. My hands trembled like I remember my great-grandmother's hands doing when I was young. I had terrible anxiety, and even worse memory. I startled easily and often. I had migraine headaches that lasted for days, and a heartbeat that liked to trip in a manner that got my attention, and not in a good way. It seemed that any stress put me over the edge. In short, I was a mess. Beyond the struggles with our adopted children, our family had been through a lot of loss, professionally and personally. It had been a very tough three years, and through I had 'done the work' with God, my body still took the hit. My doctor gave me instruction to listen closely and write down his words: "the body never lies, and the body always wins." Among other things he said that day, my take-a-way was that I cannot over-ride my body with my strong determination. To only focus on the needs of my children, without caring for my physical well-being, is dangerous.

We are fearfully and wonderfully made. God has hardwired us to require food, exercise, and touch. They are all part of His grand plan, to help us live in and enjoy this world. I had to learn that even though I don't want my physical self to lead, I also don't want it to drag the other parts of myself down. So can I encourage you (and myself) to go for a walk, get a massage, take your vitamins, and learn to enjoy healthy real food? Stop trying to be self-sufficient and negligent. Maybe no one has ever taken good care of you, and this whole idea of self-care is very foreign to you. There's no better time than the present to learn.

Remember, this parenting thing is a marathon, not a sprint, and you need to get moving. Practicing self-care is the first step toward putting on your "oxygen mask" first, so you can take care of your children for the long term.

Soul

We must guard what we feed our souls, being vigilant about what we allow into our head through what we watch on TV, what we see on the computer, and what erroneous thoughts we allow our mind to dwell on. There is nothing inherently wrong with a movie or facebook, but the danger comes in how subtly they influence our thoughts. What might be perfectly permissible for someone else, might be a land-mine for you. Use your best judgment and common sense.

If reading other families' adoption blogs leaves you depressed and discontent because the grass seems so much greener over there, then stop feeding your mind with that information. Most parents of children in need of their own healing, are themselves mentally exhausted and need a break. One of the best ways I've found to balance my sometimes crazy up-and-down emotional world, is to look for simple joy. It may sound trite, but it's powerful. When life is feeling particularly out of control, look for ways to feel like you've accomplished order. Make the bed, clean your bathroom, or take a shower. Do things that bring delight to your senses. Find what brings you happiness, no matter how small it might be. (Of course, this requires that you are able to practice self-compassion, and reject perfection). Create. Cook. Paint. Play. Maybe you take pleasure in cuddling your dog, drawing a picture, or swinging in your backyard. Maybe you burn a candle, intentionally stare at a beautiful sky, listen to your favorite music, or give your spouse a long hug. Do whatever works, to help bring you into a creative and calm state.

Find ways to laugh, and safe people you can laugh with. Research has proven the importance of drinking water, taking fish oil, meditation, exercise, and eating right. While all these are true and good ideas, it's important you discover the things that are personally fun for you. No one else can tell you what delights you; only you know. For me it's varied from Israeli dancing, to painting with my kids, to cranking up the music of Chaka Kahn! Yes, with the windows down, 'I'm every woman!' When the only progress it seems you make is by moving one inch at a time, it's time for you to step back and ask for a fresh perspective. My Pastor used to tell a joke, "What did the snail say on the back of a turtle?" He loved squealing the answer with a high-pitched, "Wheeee!"

Getting a fresh perspective will do wonders for your mental health. Make time to do things that help you step back, take a deep breath, and remove yourself from the mental haze. Go for a drive, call a friend, or go on a walk. Conversation with a wise and trusted friend is a wonderful way to find fresh perspective. I love talking to the elderly; they have so much to share and have made it through many difficult seasons in their own lives. Hearing from them helps me keep in mind that "this too, shall pass" and we will make it to a later stage of life. Ask yourself clarifying questions to blow away the fog. What do we want to remember? What do we want our children to remember?

There are other creative ways you can promote emotional health. My dad taught my sisters and I to de-stress with a primal scream. In the car, he would tell us, "Hey, on three, we're all going to let our psyche out." I'm not really sure he used that word properly, but the count would begin, and then all of us would scream at the top of our lungs. It makes me laugh even thinking about it now, but it's something I do with my kids from time to time. Give it a try, it feels pretty great!

It's important during extended periods of stress that you go easy on yourself. You may find your memory is not as clear, and recall is difficult at times. This is a sign you need to give yourself permission to slow down, and keep your commitments to others at a minimum.

Find others who are willing to share your burdens. I strongly believe it is imperative for you to connect in a local church body. The enemy wants nothing more than to get you isolated and alone, so he can wreak havoc in your life. Do not allow him to separate you from a body of believers. Like a lion that first isolates the gazelle from her flock, you will be left open to attack if you remove yourself from the covering of a church family. This family should feel like your safe place, not another arena where you have to pretend to be perfect. If you can't be real there, keep moving until you find the right church home. Being rooted is vital to growth. It is important that you put down roots where your family can be strengthened and supported. Be wary of legalistic mindsets that would demand obedience from you and your children. Instead, look for those who lead with grace and love.

I have been blessed to find other women within my church community to pray with regularly. Sometimes it's hard to ask for prayer, as I am still a recovering perfectionist with a lot of pride. I do it though. I don't share every detail, because it isn't always necessary, and I want to protect the privacy of my children. I found I can ask for what I need without going into specifics about each situation. For example, I have asked, "Please pray that God would give me a soft heart toward my children" instead of sharing how at this time they are lying all the time, hoarding food, and attempting to manipulate at every opportunity. Identify the safe people in your life who can support you well. I have found one friend with whom I can be completely honest and vulnerable with. She is my partner in prayer, and the one who stands with me in hope. It has been vital for me to have someone who will challenge me in my walk, and lift me up in so many ways. I recommend you keep the list of people you are completely 100% transparent and vulnerable with short. You don't need ten friends who can fill this role; only one or two you know you can count on.

Practice gratitude regularly. So much of our joy or stress is influenced by our perspective. Set yours to what is going right, and count your blessings one by one. When your mind begins to ruminate, and it will, bring it back to the present and shift focus on those things that you are grateful for in your life. I recently had a client that was fearful of having her wisdom teeth pulled. She was so afraid that she was having panic attacks two weeks prior to the procedure. She was being robbed of her present experience by fear of the future. Through our discussion she was able to change her focus from all that could go wrong, to being grateful for all that was right. For example, she gave thanks that she lives in America, and has access to trained dental staff, a clean dental office, modern sterilized equipment, and Novocain!

As I mentioned earlier, it is important to find ways to stay present. Through breath and mindfulness practices, we have a much greater opportunity to fully engage and connect with what God is doing in our lives at this very moment. If we follow Christ's teaching, we will learn to be more present, thus finding our way at a manageable pace. "So do not worry about tomorrow; for tomorrow will care for itself. Each day has enough trouble of its own." (Matthew 6:24, NLT)

Spirit

There are only so many hours in the day. We must choose to use them wisely, and fuel the engine that sustains us. So, how do we engage successfully? By choosing to stand in victory and empowering our spirit to have faith. We know that "faith comes from hearing, that is, hearing the Good News about Christ." (Romans 10:17, NLT) Our spirit is uplifted and edified when we are in God's word. We must actively pursue the truth with time spent in scripture. It is also important to train your longings and your "flesh" helping place them under the authority of your spirit. This will take discipline, and there is nothing that will help you develop this discipline better than prayer and fasting. Denying the cravings of our physical body and soul through fasting, opens a clear pathway for us to hear the quiet directives of the spirit. By definition, fasting means giving up something pleasurable with the intentional mindset of desiring God more than you long for the thing you are denying. While food is what we normally associate giving up for a fast, you aren't limited to it. Whatever you give up needs to be personal to you. It may be social media, TV, or coffee.

There are books upon books written about fasting, (I recommend Jentezen Franklin's). The bottom line is, fasting as a discipline facilitates breakthrough in tough areas of your life where you are facing heavy warfare. In Mark chapter 9, we read as Jesus is talking to his disciples after they had not had success with a deaf and dumb spirit. His disciples asked Him privately, "Why could we not cast it out?" So He said to them, "This kind can come out by nothing but prayer and fasting." (Mark 9: 23-29, NKJV) It would appear that there are just some situations that require fasting in order to secure the victory. As parents, we desperately want so much for our children. We say that "our ceiling will be their floor." When it comes down to it though, what are we actually doing now to make that dream a reality? It takes great intentionality to our children and what they need, modeling parenting we ourselves may not have experienced.

Even if we had amazing parents, they were human and not perfect. Yet, we do have a perfect Father who loves us and gave us His Son, so we would have the ability to parent our children the way He has called us to. When we don't know what to do, we can turn to Him for answers. When we have nothing left to give, we can draw from the deep well of His grace. By surrendering our spirit to His truth in prayer, we are empowered to manage our thoughts and are equipped with all we need, to be the parent our children so desperately need.

As Philippians 4:6 reads, "Don't worry about anything; instead, pray about everything. Tell God what you need, and thank him for all he has done." (Philippians 4:6, NLT) Directing our thoughts toward God in prayer is an excellent way of taking our thoughts captive and submitting our mind and emotions to Him. While it is vital for us to have a personal prayer life, there's something powerful about parents uniting in prayer for their children. There was a time that my husband and I would frequently go on long prayer walks together through our neighborhood. With all we had going on, it was sometimes ten p.m. before we had time, but the walks were always well worth it. Yes, we did a little venting and even engaged in sarcastic humor about parenting. Yet, we found that the most helpful thing for us to do for our kids, was to pray together. We were not polished, just real and honest with God, acknowledging our failures and imploring Him for help. In doing so, we shifted our focus from the problem or challenge and onto God, our hope and solution.

Three in One

I was raised in a Jewish home and came to believe in Jesus, YeShua, in college. Throughout my childhood I recited the ancient prayer, the Shema, acknowledging God as "Adonai Echad" or "Lord, Three in One." Growing up I never thought to ask what it meant that His name included Echad, but as a Jewish believer, I think it is pretty cool. While God is One, I have found it a valuable practice to talk to each of His three persons separately, developing a relationship with the Father, the Son, and the Holy Spirit. As Christians, it's common enough to hear people say they have "invited God into their hearts." But what does that look like in the context of healing our childhoods, and parenting emotionally injured kids? Is it merely some platitude, or is there real power to succeed in that invitation? I believe that if we want to see real change come about from asking God to invade our hearts, we must invite Him in with the intention of giving Him full control over all we are, and all we do. Like Paul writes, "My old self has been crucified with Christ. It is no longer I who lives, but Christ lives in me. So I live in this earthly body by trusting in the Son of God, who loved me and gave himself for me." (Galatians 2:20, NLT) In this surrender, we submit our whole lives, choosing to no longer operate according to our will and way. If we do this, we will find that when it comes to our children, we respond more according to their needs and histories, and react less from ours.

Our God is endless, and there is no limit to His attributes. The longer we are in a relationship with Him, the more intimately we can come to know different facets of who He is, although we will never fully understand Him. God desires to reveal more of who He is to us, but it is up to us to pursue that knowledge. You may find it easiest to talk to Jesus, or maybe the Holy Spirit. Start wherever you feel most comfortable. As far as method goes, the Bible simply tells us to worship God in spirit and truth. "God is Spirit, and those who worship Him must worship in spirit and truth." (John 4:24, NLT) We must allow ourselves the opportunity to do just that. Use the truth of scripture, your prayer language, song, dance, or any other way you can worship Him sincerely. It doesn't have to be liturgical, rehearsed, or fancy. We simply need to be ourselves. He already loves us and knows us fully. We need to just come as we are and talk to Him.

Here are some ideas of how you can talk to each member of the Godhead:

Father

Acknowledge God the Father as the Creator of the Universe, who is the same yesterday, today, and forever. Give Him praise for all he has done in our world and in your life. Meditate on His goodness. Thank Him for being a loving Father who cares intimately for His children.

Son

Worship Jesus the Son for His obedience and sacrifice. Praise Him for the power found in His blood. Thank Him for making a way for us to access the Father, and for interceding for each of us that belong to Him.

Holy Spirit

Praise the Holy Spirit for being your help-mate. Thank Him for never leaving you, and for giving you guidance. Thank Him for the many gifts of His Spirit, enabling you to have victory in your life.

Like any relationship, we will get to know God better as we invest our time, and begin to risk our heart with Him. Remember, that we must not be double minded, but confident and full of faith when we come to God in prayer.

As James writes, "When you ask him, be sure that your faith is in God alone. Do not waver, for a person with divided loyalty is as unsettled as a wave of the sea that is blown and tossed by the wind. Such people should not expect to receive anything from the Lord. Their loyalty is divided between God and the world, and they are unstable in everything they do." (James 1:6-8, NLT) We will find power in our prayer when we pray the word of God, "for the word of God is alive and powerful. It is sharper than the sharpest two-edged sword, cutting between soul and spirit, between joint and marrow. It exposes our innermost thoughts and desires." (Hebrews 4:12, NLT) When we do, we know that our prayers will accomplish that which they are set out to do as God's word does not return void. Our prayers are active and will work to change things according to God's purpose and glory. His word tells us in Isaiah 55:11 "It is the same with my word. I send it out, and it always produces fruit. It will accomplish all I want it to, and it will prosper everywhere I send it."

Chapter 6 Study

You are What You Eat

"To bestow on them a crown of beauty instead of ashes, the oil of gladness instead of mourning, and a garment of praise instead of a spirit of despair" (Isaiah 61:1-3, NLT)

.

Read Isaiah 61: 1-3. Where do you find yourself? Take a moment to pray, asking God to lead you through the following questions.

1. Explain how you have been poor in spirit.

2. Where are you in darkness? What has held you captive?

3. Do you believe God can comfort you in a lasting way? Do you believe you deserve to be comforted? Explain.

4. Please read Matthew 9:27-29, Luke 8:42-48. What one thing did all these people have in order to be healed?

We too, can become accustomed to our brokenness, our captivity, and our grief. Just as Christ was with the crippled man, He is with us. When we are lacking faith, He often asks us to take a step to display it.

5. What action step is Christ asking of you in order that you might be healed?

6. What examples of humility can you relate to with regard to parenting?

7. Is there anyone that you need to forgive, whether they deserve it or not?

8. What are some of your favorite qualities of the Lord that you admire?

9. What is one declaration you would like to proclaim over your situation?

Chapter 7

Something about that Name

"My daughter has night terrors waking us regularly at four a.m. . . . A tiny baby, she has worn us down with her screams. We are reduced to heaps of useless, tired flesh, often pointing fingers at each other for ruining our once peaceful lives."

-Joseph, P.

"There's just something about that name"

Jesus

I love the song *There's Something About that Name* by Bill and Gloria Gaither. There is something about the name Jesus because there is power in His identity. He is alive in us and working on our behalf. In many ways, He is a great mystery for our minds to conceive.

However, our spirit understands and if we let it have power over our mind, we can speak victoriously to our circumstances, feelings, and thoughts. Spirit Managed Living means we pull down useless imaginations and bring every thought captive in submission to the truth, which is Jesus. "For the weapons of our warfare are not carnal but mighty in God for pulling down strongholds, casting down arguments and every high thing that exalts itself against the knowledge of God, bringing every thought into captivity to the obedience of Christ, and being ready to punish all disobedience when your obedience is fulfilled." (2 Corinthians 10:4-6, NKJV)

As believers, we have invited the Holy Spirit to live within us. Unlike those walking apart from Christ, our spirits have holy guidance from the one true God who desires us to live in fellowship and communion with Him. He is longing for us to talk to Him, and is waiting to assist us the moment we invite Him in to our every moment and situation. The best part is we don't need to go anywhere to find Him. He is already right here. And while we all know that, there are those times it seems He's nowhere to be found. For those times, there are things we can do to train ourselves to hear Him more clearly, and access His strength more completely. As we practice these things, like a dimmer switch slowly releasing more light, we will begin to see our "house" become brighter as more of the Holy Spirit is allowed to shine in our hearts and lives.

According to Scripture, the fruit of the Spirit is love, joy, peace, long-suffering, kindness, goodness, faithfulness, gentleness, and self-control. (Galatians 5:22-23, NLT) These are the qualities our parenting should emulate. When we choose to heal kids with pain and brokenness in their histories, we bring the battlefield straight into our own home. We become warriors, and should take to heart the instructions to put on the full armor of God. We read, "Be strong in the Lord and in his mighty power. Put on all of God's armor so that you will be able to stand firm against all strategies of the devil. For we are not fighting against flesh-and-blood enemies, but against evil rulers and authorities of the unseen world, against mighty powers in this dark world, and against evil spirits in the heavenly places. Therefore, put on every piece of God's armor so you will be able to resist the enemy in the time of evil. Then after the battle you will still be standing firm." (Ephesians 6:10-13, NLT) There is much to learn if we are to fight effectively!

Fighting in the strength of the Holy Spirit gives us the upper hand in this war. He is the one who will instruct us in every challenge. As David wrote, "Praise the Lord, who is my rock. He trains my hands for war and gives my fingers skill for battle." (Psalm 144:1, NLT) The Lord will provide us the strategies to overcome any attack the enemy sends our way. We need to prepare our hearts and minds to take that instruction. Can you see yourself acting from God's instruction, instead of reacting in your own thoughts and emotion? The Bible teaches that, "When people do not accept divine guidance, they run wild. But whoever obeys the law is joyful." (Proverbs 29:18, NLT) It's time for us to accept His guidance and become the parents our children need us to be. To do so we need a vision and a goal. What does victory look like? Who do you need to be in order to win the battle before you? Our minds must see ourselves the way the Holy Spirit sees us. Now that we've placed Him in charge, it's time we get on the same page as Him. And what is the image of how He sees us? It is the picture of a parent warrior, fighting with the truth of God's Word, from His divine guidance, in a manner that displays the fruit of God's Holy Spirit. It is a warrior who recognizes all strength and love come from God. A warrior who knows they can effectively give strength and love to their children, when they have spent time receiving it for themselves.

When we are able to get an accurate picture of ourselves as children of God, we can begin to picture a victorious outcome for our children and do our part to secure it. Our brains will fight us. In every situation our brains will want to find immediate resolve and direction. Remember, the brain longs to be in charge, and will tell us to react as past experiences have trained it to do. Yet we can re-train the brain to focus on our vision instead of our fear. Dr. Waggoner encourages others to clarify their vision with three words of their choice. For example, my vision was to be poised, compassionate, and faith-driven. When my brain wanted to react to any given situation I would try to quiet myself with a cleansing breath and repeat in my mind, "I am poised, compassionate, and equipped with God's word." I would use this routine to help quiet my brain and give time for my spirit to take in God's direction instead. I also used Dr. Dan Hughes model of parenting from a safe PLACE (playful, loving, accepting, curious, and empathic) to help me hit 'reset' before I interacted with my kids. Again, having a vision for who I wanted to be helped me act and not react. It also helped me prepare my mind to be receptive to God's voice while dethroning my reactive brain. The most important part of this exercise however, was that it allowed me as a parent to take a moment to ask God to reveal what is going on inside of me. Most often it was feelings of being out of control and fear that the chaos may never end. Immediately, I could see the target and I could then ask for His help. I would realize, "Oh, my brain wants control and I am battling lies of fear and dread . . . second verse same as the first!" I could come to Him then as a child and ask for help, knowing where I was in trouble. This process isn't easy and certainly doesn't feel natural at first, but when we have a target to aim for, it is much more likely that we will reach the goal.

Humility

I believe the process of living with a new vision begins with humility. By humility, we are able to say, "I'm wrong," "I don't know," and "I'm sorry." These are phrases that may not come naturally to some of us; in fact, they might grate on our every last nerve. Some of us weren't given examples of how to do this as we were growing up, and we have a tough time admitting when we don't know the answer or when we are wrong. It's another lie of the Orphan Mindset, telling us that to be wrong is to be a failure, and that to not know something, admits vulnerability or weakness. The adversary wants us to believe humility is equal to being "less than" and to be less than is the same as being rejected. Jesus on the other hand, tells us to come like little children. He calls us His sheep and gently reminds us over and over that humility is a position of deep strength. In humility, we find access to and gain His strength instead of our own feeble strength.

The first way we show our humility and dependence on God is by having a repentant heart. When our hearts are humble and repentant, we can honestly see our flaws and quickly say "I'm sorry." Not only do we need this ability to apologize to each other, but even more importantly we must be able to truly repent before God. I believe it's important to begin our prayers with an acknowledgement of our sins and mistakes, to remove any barriers that would hinder the rest of our prayer from being heard. I don't mean a long laundry list of trying to apologize for every single thing, real or imagined. I mean genuinely approaching God simply with a heart that cries out, "I am a little child before You who has blown it again. I'm sorry. I am in desperate need of You." In the Bible, Jesus often uses the picture of a Shepherd and his sheep to describe the relationship we have with Him. The power of this analogy is often lost on many of us, as we don't have the agricultural background allowing us to understand the intricacies of the parallel. With a little digging though, the picture comes to life. I have been told that when sheep have ear mites, they are driven to hit their head against a tree over and over again, in an attempt to find relief. It doesn't solve the problem, and the sheep are dumb enough they could actually injure themselves by trying. How like me! There have been so many times I've wanted to bang my head against a wall because nothing I try seems to make a lasting impact with my kids. I come to the Lord saying, "Father, I am so angry. I am just a stupid little lamb and I have lost my temper again. I am not who I want to be. Please erase the memories of my children for today's situation, and help me start over."

After making things right with our heavenly Father, it is vital that we make reparation with our children. If you're like me, you may find yourself apologizing to your kids more times in one week than you have received in a lifetime. It will be uncomfortable. You may not have grown up in a family that modeled humble parenting. The importance in this action is how we illustrate to our children the world doesn't fall apart when we make mistakes, and that we are worthy of an apology. Humility removes the pressure for perfection. By showing your kids their parents aren't perfect, you give them (and yourself) permission to stop striving for perfection. What a relief!

Forgiveness

After asking forgiveness from God and my children, I've found it's important to examine my heart for any unforgiveness I might be harboring toward others. Even after I have consciously chosen to forgive in the past, like a stowaway on a ship, resentment has a way of sneaking unforgiveness back on board. A lot of adoptive parents have shared that they have been abandoned in one way or another from those they needed most. Family members, friends, and the church body have made cruel judgements, critical statements, and at times, acted with complete apathy. Consider for example, how much anger and hurt is present when one feels misunderstood. In the aftermath, it's one thing to forgive the people involved when you are operating from a position of strength; it's an altogether different thing to forgive when you're battling a raging child, exhausted mentally, physically, and emotionally. When you really long for compassion, connection and grace, and it is nowhere to be found, it's painful. Forgiveness is harder then. In that moment, your adversary sweeps in with thoughts reminding you of the faces and names of those who have hurt you, left you, and betrayed you.

Our enemy knows the Scripture, and he knows Jesus' words were recorded when He said, "If you forgive those who sin against you, your heavenly Father will forgive you. But if you refuse to forgive others, your Father will not forgive your sins." (Matthew 6:14-15, NLT) Satan wants to keep us in unforgiveness because he knows our prayers are rendered ineffective as we have compromised our authority. Recall the story of the Good Samaritan. You, like the man attacked by bandits, may feel as though you were left for dead on the side of the road, ignored by your own "people" who should have stopped to help you. Bleeding and helpless, they take everything you have to give, and relish in their spoils. Others walk by and keep on walking. The scene of you and your troubles is too much for them to believe or involve themselves in. You try to reconcile the reality of your situation and make sense of it, but you cannot. Even then, when nothing makes sense and you have done nothing wrong, forgiveness is necessary.

Extending forgiveness does not negate what has been done to you, but it will release you from the all-consuming drive to understand it. You may feel alone, but God will be there for you. Though it will be hard to trust again, He will bring along a "Good Samaritan" to pull you out of your ditch and help you mend. At some point it will be vital to not only mentally forgive those who have hurt you, express it verbally to the Lord. Forgiveness is an action word, not just a mental state. You can't just simply say, "Oh yeah, I forgive them. It is what it is." It is important to take stock of the hurt and offense before you hand it over to the Lord. Even if you don't feel like you have forgiven, the Lord longs to hear that you make the conscious choice to do so anyway. It is this acknowledgement that draws you closer to Him. He can then be your defense, and you have shown willingness to rest in Him, letting go of self-reliance. Consider David who cried, "He alone is my rock and my salvation, my fortress where I will not be shaken. My victory and honor come from God alone. He is my refuge, a rock where no enemy can reach me." (Psalm 62: 6-7, NLT)

I love how Marty Geotz put these verses to song singing, "He is my defense, I shall not be moved." (Marty Geotz, Singing in the Reign Music, 1986) The one who hurt you may have very little desire or motivation to reconcile, and may not even be a safe person for you to attempt reconciliation. You may wisely choose to extend forgiveness only in private prayer. The point of extending forgiveness is so you can be released from the torment and prison of unforgiveness and move forward. It's an act of obedience that carries no expectation of others with it. When you take a stand on forgiveness, you send a clear signal to the Lord that you trust Him alone, acknowledging He is your Shelter, Strong Tower, and Ever-Present Help in time of trouble. By your actions, you communicate to Him that you recognize and believe His sacrifice on the Cross was sufficient to cover all sin, both yours and theirs. Forgiveness underlines this belief, and gives you eyes to see your offenders through the covering of Christ. This simple act clears the static noise of the enemy, who in all he does strives to keep your focus on your pain and off your God. Make no mistake, the offense will try to perform on the stage of your mind again and again. Just mentally picture a hook to remove the bad act, and remind yourself that the show is over.

Acknowledge and Adore

When you have acknowledged the pardoning of your own sin and the sins of others through humility and forgiveness, you are in a place to offer sincere worship. Distractions have been removed, and it is time for your soul to acknowledge and adore the Lord. Worship is a powerful battle position. In the stillness of our soul, we become strong in faith by meditating on who God is, and praising Him for it. God already knows who He is, so you aren't telling Him anything new; but He loves to hear it from us. Repeating out loud who God is deposits truth into our spirit and mind, building our faith in the process.

Proclaim and Declare

Remember, the fruit of the Holy Spirit is love, joy, peace, patience, kindness, goodness, gentleness, and self-control. (Galatians 5:22-23, NLT) These things are yours by right of your inheritance as children of God. Watch your words, remember you are not what you feel, and declare by faith you are full of the fruit of the Spirit.

One of my favorite movies when I was younger was The Princess Bride. I have always loved the scene when Inigo Montoya has met his lifelong enemy, and states his name and intention: "My name is Inigo Montoya; you killed my father, prepare to die." Sometimes it is in our best interest to clearly state our name and intention with all the courage this character portrayed. We remember our identity in Christ, believing His blood covers all, and we do have the victory. Read the following sentence out loud, putting your name in the blank, and declare it over your life:

"I am _____, daughter/son of the Most High God, prepare to live!"

After acknowledging and adoring God for who He is, your spirit will be charged by the truth you have been speaking aloud. Now is your time to stand on that truth, speaking life and hope into your situation. The Lord already knows all the details about your circumstances; it isn't necessary to go on and on rehearsing everything that is wrong about your life. Be honest, but spend more time inviting Him in and proclaiming truth, than you do recanting all your woes. This may sound something like: "Lord, I know You are aware, even more than I am, of my family's needs. Thank You for longing to care for us. Thank You for being the God who has cattle on a thousand hills to provide for all our needs. Lord, we declare that good things are coming our way. We proclaim that we are the head and not the tail. We have victory and not confusion. We are calling in provision and healing for our family. We thank You that your gifts are given in good measure, pressed down, shaken together, and flowing over. Nothing is impossible for You, Lord. Thank You Father that we can rest in You, our lives and our futures are secure."

In closing, the words that come to mind are: lather, rinse, repeat! While much of what has been written in this little book is practical advice, it is my opinion that it is better taken as a lifestyle, rather than some quick acting formula for success. It is my hope that you have been given some things to ponder with regard to expectations, core beliefs, and strategies for living. It is my sincere desire that you stay engaged in your own process of healing and growth so that you will be able to offer parenting that restores the heart of a child. When you accept that you are loved beyond measure, you will be able to offer love beyond measure. And those two acts will change the world!

Chapter 7 Study
Something about that Name

Old Testament names for God

- ELOHIM - Genesis 1:1, Psalm 19:1 - meaning "God", a reference to God's power and might.

- ADONAI - Malachi 1:6 - meaning "Lord", a reference to the Lordship of God.

- JEHOVAH—YAHWEH - Genesis 2:4 – a reference to God's divine salvation.

- JEHOVAH-MACCADDESHEM - Exodus 31:13 - meaning "The Lord thy sanctifier"

- JEHOVAH-ROHI - Psalm 23:1 - meaning "The Lord my shepherd"

- JEHOVAH-SHAMMAH - Ezekiel 48:35 - meaning "The Lord who is present"

- JEHOVAH-RAPHA - Exodus 15:26 - meaning "The Lord our healer"

- JEHOVAH-TSIDKENU - Jeremiah 23:6 - meaning "The Lord our righteousness"

- JEHOVAH-JIREH – Genesis 22:13-14 - meaning "The Lord will provide"

- JEHOVAH-NISSI - Exodus 17:15 - meaning "The Lord our banner"

- JEHOVAH-SHALOM - Judges 6:24 - meaning "The Lord is peace"

- JEHOVAH-SABBAOTH - Isaiah 6:1-3 - meaning "The Lord of Hosts"

- JEHOVAH-GMOLAH - Jeremiah 51:6 - meaning "The God of Recompense"

- EL-ELYON - Genesis 14:17-20, Isaiah 14:13-14 - meaning "The most high God"

- EL-ROI - Genesis 16:13 - meaning "The strong one who sees"

- EL-SHADDAI - Genesis 17:1, Psalm 91:1 - meaning "The God of the mountains or God Almighty"

- EL-OLAM - Isaiah 40:28-31 – meaning "The everlasting God"

1. What name and attribute of God draws you in at this season of your life? What is it about that name?

2. What is a special name God has for you?

3. Is there one new way that you can see yourself the way God sees you?

4. Write an action plan for Self-Care. Consider ways that you can show Self Compassion and find balance in your life. What are some tangible ways you can set action steps to this vision?

5. What is your plan for ongoing connection?

Notes

References

Holy Bible as noted in copyright

Man's Search for Meaning (1946) Viktor Frankl

Adopting the Hurt Child (1995) Keck, Gregory, C., Ph.D. and Kupecky, Regina, M., LCSW

The Connected Child (2007) By: Karyn B. Purvis, David R. Cross, Wendy Sunshine

Living Confidently Out of Your Mind (2011) Ron Waggoner, Ph.D.

Abroad & Back (2003) Keck, Gregory, C., Ph.D. and Kupecky, Regina, M., LCSW

Attaching in Adoption (2001) Gray, Deborah, Ph.D.

Dyadic Developmental Psychotherapy is a treatment developed by Daniel Hughes, Ph.D., (Hughes, 2008, Hughes, 2006, Hughes, 2003,).

www.dyadicdevelopmentalpsychotherapy.org

The Association for Treatment and Training in the Attachment of Children

(ATTACH) www.attach.org

CPSIA information can be obtained
at www.ICGtesting.com
Printed in the USA
BVHW090848180322
631653BV00001B/100